Before You Divorce

Before You Divorce

James Edmeade

Abbreviations of other Bible versions used:

NASB = New American Standard Bible
NEB = New English Bible
NIV = New International Version
NKJ = New King James
NWT = New World Translation
RSV = Revised Standard Version
TLB = The Living Bible

Companion Press
P.O. Box 310
Shippensburg, PA 17257

"Good Stewards of the
Manifold Grace of God"

ISBN 1-56043-505-4

For Worldwide Distribution
Printed in the U.S.A.

Contents

A Word of Thanks

My personal thanks to Pastor Lynford Williams, who donated some of the materials for this book. To my sons-in-law, Pastors Ruthven Roy and Eric Bell, who provided some of the inspiration and motivation for the task. My thanks also to Mr. Bertram Baly, Mr. and Mrs. Frederick Lettsome, Pastor Carlton Williams of Zion Assembly, Pastor Charles Peters, District Superintendent of the Moravian Churches in the Virgin Islands, Mrs. Naomi King, Mr. Mervin Rogers who helped with the proofreading, Breaklight Business Services which typed the original manuscripts, and my wife, Veronica, who assisted with the preparations in one way or another.

To the Reader

You will observe that I have tried to avoid the use of meaningless slogans, big words, and ambiguous phrases. I want to give you an opportunity to focus primarily upon the subject matter, rather than on the literary style or classics of my work.

As soon as you have read and carefully studied the book, please feel free to call or write to me, expressing your personal opinions and evaluation of my work. Your comments on this publication will be greatly appreciated.

James Edmeade, Author
P.O. Box 10428
St. Thomas
U.S. Virgin Islands 00801
(Tel. 809-775-1239)

Foreword

In December of 1987, my wife and I spent a most enjoyable evening in the home of a young energetic married couple. A few of their friends had come over to study the Bible with them. After a very lively and interesting Bible study, we ended the evening with a heated debate over divorce and remarriage. Yet, we left with many important questions still unanswered.

I decided, then, to pursue the issue further. I had not thought of writing a book on the subject; my interest was simply to become better acquainted with and more informed on the issue and, ultimately, to provide answers to some of the more perplexing questions that often haunt married couples. But it soon became evident that a book would be helpful in passing on the full benefits of my research to as many persons as possible.

When I told a friend that I, a layperson, was about to write a book on divorce and remarriage, his initial response was "What, man, that's heavy stuff." Another queried, "What does he really know about the subject to be writing a book?" A third grumbled, "I thought only professionals could handle such things."

Although I agree in principle with all of these assessments and assumptions, I was not discouraged by these remarks. As a layperson, I had vowed to enter this debate not to draw attention to myself, but because I felt confident that I could make a positive contribution to this matter of divorce and remarriage. I wish that more laypeople would take their position and join with the professionals in speaking out boldly, and yes, even writing, on these serious issues that affect the lives of our people.

No one knows better than I that logic and humanistic considerations alone cannot handle problems as deep and complex as divorce and remarriage. Spiritual ills demand spiritual therapy. The Bible, God's Word, is the fundamental medicine for all of man's maladies. That is where we must look for solutions to our marital problems. Although the sociologists, psychologists, and other secular workers may offer valuable assistance and practical solutions to serious problems, these people are themselves often the victims of some peculiar circumstances from which they are wholly unable to free themselves.

Some time ago I visited the home of a young psychologist in New York City. He worked as a counselor in a large hospital, but had just moved to live by himself in his newly established home. Conversing with him, I plugged this question: "Sir, what of the people who come to your clinic from time to time for counselling? Are you always able to help them find solutions to their problems?" He replied, "Sometimes they come to me with their family difficulties, but I just don't know what to tell them, because I, too, have my own family troubles." He had recently divorced.

Divorce is an epidemic that is gradually eating away the moral and spiritual fabric of society. Our homes are under fire. Divorce is a way of life for many, and its easy acceptance by even the clergy has clothed it with an aura of respectability it does not deserve. Divorce has inflicted endless suffering and sleepless nights upon many families. Its impact upon society and the church has been disastrous. Saddest of all is the fact that statistics show children to be the worst victims of this social anomaly. Yet in some countries all it takes is a few dollars to secure a divorce and destroy a marriage. But divorce is nothing really new. Moses legalized it, Jesus discussed it, and Paul, perhaps the most ardent advocate of a stable marriage, tolerated it. (See First Corinthians 7:1-15.) Today church members and ministers alike are getting divorced.

On a popular talk show, a deserted man, in agony, described his dilemma. Sick and losing weight, he told how his wife, whom he apparently loved with a passion, had run off to live with another man. She had left behind only a short note warning him not to divorce her, for in it she said, "I will be back home as soon as possible after I've received my new experience."

Adultery is madness of the highest order, against God and against one's self (1 Cor. 6:18).

If this book can in any way help stop this madness; if it shows the villainy and hopelessness of sin; if it causes some soul to ponder, and upon reflecting to choose the more reasonable course of prudence and sanity in dealing with family problems; then my living shall not be in vain. If by my work some husband or wife is led to inquire, "Lord, am I doing my best to make my marriage a success?" If it stimulates one to become the model parent that his or her children can respect; if it helps some intolerant husband, or some boisterous wife to be reasonable and calm down, some immoral person to be pure, if it encourages some distressed mate to look to the God of all comfort for solace and grace in times of stress and conflict, then truly my work shall not be in vain. If it leads to such self-examination that a man or a woman will ask, "Lord, am I the kind of loving, caring, husband or wife others think I am? Or am I engaging in show business, the art of making impressions?" If it stirs one enough to inquire, "Lord in the day of judgment, when the secrets of all hearts shall be disclosed, will I be able to pass the scrutiny of Heaven, Your holiness test?" Then the book has accomplished its purpose.

It is my prayer that this book will encourage some husband or wife to learn the art of peacefully living together, without the trauma of divorce and separation; that it will bring deliverance and salvation to troubled hearts and troubled homes; and ultimately, that God will be glorified.

James Edmeade
Author

Personal Profile

HOW WE ESCAPED DIVORCE

Early in our marriage my wife and I discovered that marital happiness and tranquility can be maintained and difficulties resolved peacefully if both spouses would be reasonable and always act with a sense of responsibility. Selfishness is nearly always the greatest hindrance to the quick resolution of marital problems. Once self is out of the way, reconciliation is usually possible. For us, scolding and blaming each other did not work. When difficulties which could have had serious consequences arose, my wife and I would simply refuse to fret or scold. Instead we waited patiently for the proper time and place to resolve our differences.

Sitting alone in our parked car was often the ideal setting for resolving conflicts. There in quiet solitude we would air our differences, each giving the other sufficient time to present his or her grievances without interruption. After the confrontation was all over and the matter thoroughly threshed out and resolved, feelings of joy and acceptance would break over us like the waves of the sea, subduing tempers and mellowing emotions.

Another victory had been won, not for us or for self, but for Christ and good ol' common sense. At that point we would bow in prayer, thanking God for having wrought such a mighty victory on our behalf. We prayed earnestly for grace to love each other better and to place all bitterness behind us.

Of course, we are human. We are not immune to marital problems. Like all others we have had our share of wrestling with sin and self, and the battle is not over yet. But always keeping God at the center of our marriage has been the secret of our success in keeping our marital happiness through the years. We joyfully recommend this Christ-centered, practical method of resolving marital difficulties and conflicts.

Introduction

What does God think about divorce? What does the Bible teach about it? Did Jesus condemn divorce, or did He uphold it? Just what did this master teacher propound about divorce and remarriage? Is divorce a sin, and if it is, can it be forgiven? What about the apostles—Paul and the others—what did they teach on the subject?

How did early church fathers perceive the issue? Should ministers who become involved in divorcee weddings be reprimanded?

Is divorce right or wrong? Who decides? There are several books in the marketplace today on the subject of divorce and remarriage, but there is no doubt whatsoever in my mind, that this book, *Before You*

Divorce, is one of the more comprehensive and informative volumes on the subject that can be found in the U.S.

Join the debate, read it, and you will find answers to many of the questions that always puzzled you on this subject. Because one out of every two married couples eventually divorce, it is essential that we spend some time studying this unhappy phenomenon.

Chapter 1

Marriage
Without Divorce

Marriage, as an institution, has a religious history. No ancient, political civilization can claim to have invented this unique creation. God created marriage the same time He created man and woman.

FOLLOWING THE RULES

Admittedly, society has moved far beyond the ideal circumstances in which marriage and the family were first created. In a world beset by sin of every kind, none of God's perfect institutions can claim immunity from the devastating assaults of the wicked one. But, we must strive by God's grace for perfection, for a return to the ideal, and that includes our marital relationships. Married couples should not be so naive as to believe that their marriage will be a perfectly smooth ride with no hurdles to overcome and no bumps to surmount. However, there are certain essentials that, if followed, would enhance the chances of a happier and more productive marriage. The Word of God has provided guidelines that would make our homes and our marriages a success.

MARRIAGE WITH UNBELIEVERS PROHIBITED

The spiritual inequality of marriage between a believer and an unbeliever has been long established. Spiritual inequality or incompatibility results when two persons who are different at heart are bound together.

God counseled Israel:

Neither shalt thou make marriages with them [the heathen]; *thy daughter thou shalt not give unto his son, nor his daughter shalt thou take unto thy son. For they will turn away thy son from following Me, that they may serve other gods.* (Deuteronomy 7:3-4a)

With the following words the apostle Paul admonished New Testament Christians,

Be ye not unequally yoked together with unbelievers: for what fellowship hath righteousness with unrighteousness? and what communion hath light with darkness? And what concord hath Christ with Belial? or what part hath he that believeth with an infidel [or unbeliever]*?* (2 Corinthians 6:14-15)

Of His relationship with His people, God asks, "Can two walk together, except they be agreed?" (Amos 3:3) That query is appropriate also for those who would become one flesh.

"A mixed marriage is a prolific source of misery. In the course of a considerable pastoral experience I have never known one to result in perfect happiness. Believers in such unions do not level their unbelieving partners up to Christ, but are themselves dragged down to infinite misery and self reproach."[1]

Christians need to follow the guidelines set forth in the Word of God and nothing else. The saying, "When in Rome, do as the Romans do," does not apply. Just because different cultures permit loose sexual practices and sanction mixed plural marriages is no reason for Christians to let up on the demands for the moral excellence specified in the Word of God. Hiding behind a facade of custom and culture in order to violate the laws of God is both carnal and selfish. Paul warned Christians enlightened by the gospel not to practice pagan life styles and customs—not to do as the Romans do except as the Romans obey God's commandments and do what God expects of them as Romans.

This then is my word to you, and I urge it upon you in the Lord's name. Give up living like pagans with their good-for-nothing notions....because ignorance prevails among them... But that is not how you learned Christ. (Ephesians 4:17-20 NEB)

A LIFETIME COMMITMENT

Persons seeking to be married should carefully study the vows and pledges they are to take. Marrige is for keeps. Raising a family is a lifetime enterprise; there is nothing temporary or impermanent about marriage.

For the woman which hath an husband is bound by the law to her husband so long as he liveth; but if the husband be dead, she is loosed from the law of her husband. So then if, while her husband liveth, she be married to another man, she shall be called an adulteress: but if her husband be dead, she is free from that law; so that she is no adulteress, though she be married to another man. (Romans 7:2-3)

According to the apostle Paul, the woman or man who violates the law of marriage was to be branded an adulterer or adulteress. That title was to be attached to the transgressor perhaps for the rest of his or her life. Marriage was to be endured as a life and death commitment.

It was not to be entered into without preparation or a proper understanding of its nature and responsible obligations. The following quotation puts it plainly: "To gain a proper understanding of the marriage relation is *the work of a life time*. Those who marry enter a school from which they are *never in this life* to be graduated."[2]

MARRIAGE—NOT ALL HAPPINESS

Many view marriage as a symbol of happiness, and so it ought to be. Others view the relationship as a simple affair; consequently, their approach to family life is accordingly simplistic. Marriage is certainly a joyous occasion. Our Lord Himself attended a wedding in Cana of Galilee and participated in the celebrations (Jn. 2:1-2). But there is nothing simplistic about marriage. It is not all happiness and joy. In fact, marriage is sometimes more trouble in disguise than the happiness it provides. Couples begin to worry when the sweet aroma of marriage passes with the wedding day. When they begin to smell the obnoxious stench of divorce and its ugly consequences, it is then that they need to re-examine their moorings and the foundations upon which their marriage is built.

MUTUAL LOVE AND RESPECT

Let's look at the question of self-control in marriage. It is generally believed by some that a woman is to consent to her husband's sexual wishes under any circumstance, even against her personal feelings and desires. Is a woman bound to consent to her husband's carnal desires at all times? Can her sexual submission be used to keep the peace at home and to avoid marital disruptions? For any marriage to last, it must be built upon a solid foundation, not merely upon sexual intrigues and fantasy. "For other foundation can no man lay than that is laid, which is Jesus Christ" (1 Cor. 3:11). Self-control in marriage is often overlooked by some, but Paul's command in First Corinthians 10:31 should be the Christian's motto in all things: "Whether therefore ye eat, or drink, or whatsoever ye do, do all to the glory of God" (1 Cor. 10:31). Temperance and moderation should characterize all of the activities in a Christian marriage, including sexual practices.

HOW MUCH SUBMISSION

It is a mistake to imagine that with blind devotion the woman is to do exactly as her husband requires in all things, when she knows that in so doing, injury would be worked for her body and her spirit which has been ransomed from the slavery of sin. *There is one who stands higher than the husband to the wife,* it is her Redeemer and her submission to her husband is to be rendered as God has directed "as it is fit in the Lord" (Col. 3:18).[3]

"When husbands require the complete subjection of their wives declaring that women have no voice or will in the family, but must render entire submission, they place their wives in a position contrary to the scriptures."[4]

A wife's weak-natured submissiveness can have disastrous consequences for her own future. Her weakness can even lead downward to divorce. "No man can truly love his wife, when she will patiently 'submit' to become his slave...*In her passive submission she loses the value she once possessed in his eyes.*"[5] The adverse effects of unreasonable sexual submission should not be underestimated.

THE HUSBAND'S RESPONSIBILITY

God holds a husband responsible for his wife, and in the sight of God, a man's credibility depends much upon how he treats his wife. Peter's counsel to husbands cannot be lightly esteemed. "Husbands, in the same way be considerate as you live with your wives, and treat them with respect as the weaker partner and as heirs with you of the gracious gift of life, *so that nothing will hinder your prayers*" (1 Pet. 3:7 NIV).

THE RING

A physical wedding ring is of little consequence to a crumbling marriage. The joining of hearts, the little acts of kindness, of sharing, of love, are the true tokens of marriage. Holding a marriage together is a heart function. True marriage is not external. It is not the beautiful house, expensive limousine, prestigious job, or huge bank account that makes a marriage worthwhile. Some of the most harmonious and truly productive marriages are found among very poor people. Some have limited education, but they are serious individuals, totally committed to their marriage vows. Their patience with each other is exemplary. Love is the foundation of their marriage. Others may look at the outward appearance—the ring, the house, the car, etc.—but God looks at the heart, for it is in the heart that true marriage is perfected.

The idea rings throughout the Scriptures that a man and his wife are to be one flesh, not necessarily one intellect or one viewpoint, but one powerful influence; one great orchestra playing the same harmonious life tunes; one electrified, indivisible force. That is God's plan for marriage.

IT HAS NOT FAILED

Has marriage failed? Of course not. God's purpose for marriage has not failed. On the contrary, it has shown great success throughout man's anthropological history. The family structure has produced many great men and women: George Washington, Florence Nightingale, Martin Luther, Thomas Edison; the list goes on endlessly. Christ Himself was the offspring of a great family, that of Mary and Joseph with their several children. So although the family institution is sometimes plagued with problems, it has not failed and it will continue to stand the test of time. But not all marriages are successful. Statistics from even the most prudent countries show that some marriages fail while others succeed.

There is no magic formula for a perfect marriage or for marital happiness. Managing a home is not quite as easy as some think. Marriage is one of the high-stress areas of life. Jesus' disciples must have understood this well when they exclaimed, "If such is the case of the man with his wife, it is better not to marry" (Mt. 19:10 NKJ). But love for Christ is the key to success in all areas of life, including marriage. It takes total commitment to Jesus Christ, plus good ol' common sense and time.

THE REAL CAUSE OF FAILED MARRIAGES

Study the following quotations carefully.

A. "It was *Satan's* studied effort to pervert the marriage institution, to weaken its obligations and lessen its sacredness, for in no surer way could he deface the image of God in man and open the door to misery and vice."[6]

B. "*Satan* is constantly seeking to strengthen his power over the people of God by inducing them to enter into alliance with 'his' subjects."[7]

C. "Many marriages can only be productive of misery; and yet the minds of the youth run in this channel because *Satan* leads them there, making them believe that they must be married in order to be happy, when they have not the ability to control themselves or to support a family."[8]

D. "*Satan* is constantly busy hurrying inexperienced youth into marriage alliances but the less we glory in the marriages which are now taking place, the better."[9]

The following excerpt from the marriage vows is most sobering: "Be ye well assured that any who are coupled together other than as God's word doth allow, are not joined together by God, neither is their marriage lawful."

NOTES AND REFERENCES

1. W.L. Emerson, *The Bible Speaks* (Watford, Herts.: The Stanborough Press Ltd.), 377.

2. Ellen G. White, *Testimonies for the Chruch* Vol. 7, 45-48.

3. Ellen G. White, *Adventist Home,* 116.

4. Ellen G. White, Letter #18, 1891.

5. White, *Adventist Home,* 125.

6. Ellen G. White, *Patriarchs and Prophets,* 338.

7. White, *Adventist Home,* 94.

8. White, Testimonies, 121-123.

9. White, *Adventist Home,* 365, 366.

Chapter 2

Old and New Testament Moral Standards

To better understand the moral foundations beneath divorce and remarriage, let's consider a partial listing of some of the Old Testament laws and principles upon which Jewish society was founded. These high moral standards were the norm for God's people in ancient times. Although some of these laws and principles are no longer extant or the norm for Christians today, people should not doubt the exalted nature of God's laws and the high standard of moral excellence to which Christians are called, in both the Old and New Testament Scriptures.

It is the violation of these laws that impoverished and crippled our world. It is this disobedience that increased our rates of divorce and crime. The church's most crucial task, therefore, is to keep God's absolute standards of morality, purity, and perfection before the people and to uphold the true values of righteousness and holy living as the Bible teaches.

The Bible adequately addresses all the important issues that involve man's physical, social, spiritual, and economic necessities. It deals clearly with morality and immorality. Sexual matters are not censored in any way. Riedel, Tracy, and Moskowitz expressed this same viewpoint in the following words:

> In sexual matters, the Bible is both frank and explicit, to a degree that often shocks even modern readers and the range of sexual experience covered is, by almost any standard, virtually complete. From the tender and sensual Song of Solomon to the unabridged liberties of Sodom and Gomorrah, the Bible omits nothing, censors no passage because its portrayal of sex is unacceptable. The Bible is quite simply the product of a culture in which morality and honesty were valued over prudery.[1]

The following study of Old Testament standards and the New Testament's call for holiness should furnish us with a clear understanding of

God's abhorrence of sexual sin and His absolute holy and perfect nature.

OLD TESTAMENT STANDARDS

"Capital Punishment For Capital Crimes"

1. *An intruder invading another man's marriage was given the death penalty.* "If a man commits adultery with another man's wife, both the man and woman shall be put to death" (Lev. 20:10 TLB).

2. *Making sexual advances to one's stepmother was a crime.* "If a man sleeps with his father's wife, he has defiled what is his father's; both the man and the woman must die, for it is their own fault" (Lev. 20:11 TLB).

3. *Sexual deviations of every sort were condemned.* "And if a man has sexual intercourse with his daughter-in-law, both shall be executed" (Lev. 20:12 TLB).

4. *A homosexual life style was detestable.* "Where a man lies down with a male, the same as one lies down with a woman, both of them have done a detestable thing. They should be put to death without fail" (Lev. 20:13 NWT).

5. *Making sexual advances toward one's mother-in-law was deplored.* "If a man has sexual intercourse with a woman and with her mother,

it is a great evil. All three shall be burned alive to wipe out wickedness from among you" (Lev. 20:14 TLB).

6. *Sexually assaulting one's sister-in-law was forbidden.* "And if a man shall take his brother's wife, it is an unclean thing: he hath uncovered his brother's nakedness..." (Lev. 20:21).

7. *Incest was purged from the community.* "If a man has sexual intercourse with his sister, whether the daughter of his father or of his mother, it is a shameful thing, and they shall publicly be cut off from the people..." (Lev. 20:17 TLB).

8. *Sex during menstruation was forbidden.* "If a man has sexual intercourse with a woman during her period of menstruation, both shall be excommunicated, for he has uncovered her uncleaness" (Lev. 20:18 TLB).

9. *Bestiality (sex with animals) was condemned.* "If a woman has sexual intercourse with an animal, kill the woman and the animal, for they deserve their punishment" (Lev 20:16 TLB).

10. *Prostitution was outlawed.* "Do not violate your daughter's sanctity by making her a prostitute, lest the land become full of enormous wickedness" (Lev. 19:29 TLB).

11. *Spilling was punished.* "And Onan knew that the seed should not be his; and it came to pass, when he went in unto his brother's wife, that *he spilled it on the ground,* lest that he should give seed to his brother. And the thing which he did displeased the LORD, wherefore he slew him also" (Gen. 38:9-10).

12. *A man who took the virginity of a maiden was compelled to make her his wife.* "In case a man finds a girl, a virgin who has not been engaged, and he actually seizes her and lies down with her and they have been found out, the man who lay down with her must also give the girl's father fifty silver sheckels and she will become his wife due to the fact that he humiliated her. He will not be allowed to divorce her all his days" (Deut. 22:28-29 NWT).

Moses' divorce law, though somewhat liberal and easily exploited, was nonetheless stringent and prohibitive. Under this law, rapists and other sexual deviates were prohibited from further marriages. No divorce was to ever be granted these offenders.

Sex Deviates Denied Divorce

1. *Rape offenders were to never be granted a divorce.* "If a man find a damsel that is a virgin, which is not betrothed, and lay hold on her, and lie with her, and they be found; then

the man that lay with her shall give unto the damsel's father fifty shekels of silver, and she shall be his wife; because he hath humbled her, *he may not put her away* [divorce her] *all his days*" (Deut. 22:28-29).

2. *Divorce rights were denied to husbands who were scandal mongers.* "If a man marries a girl, then after sleeping with her accuses her of having had premarital intercourse with another man, saying, 'She was not a virgin when I married her,' then the girl's father and mother shall bring the proof of her virginity to the city judges. ...for he has falsely accused a virgin of Israel. *She shall remain his wife and he may never divorce her*" (Deut. 22:13-14; 19b TLB).

HOLINESS IS THE KEY

Holiness is the condition upon which all of the covenants between God and man were established. (See Leviticus 19:2; 20:7-10; and Numbers 15:40.) "I am the Lord your God who has made a distinction between you and the people of other nations. ... You shall be holy to Me, for I the Lord am holy, and I have set you apart from all other peoples to be Mine" (Lev. 20:24b,26 TLB).

God's call for holy living and His warnings against impurity have never ceased through all the centuries.

NEW TESTAMENT CALL FOR HOLINESS

The New Testament standards of morality are not identical with Old Testament norms, nor are the penalties and punishments for violations the same. For example, New Testament leaders did not practice beatings, hangings, mutilations or torture for criminal offenses, not even for murder and adultery. Such punishments formed no part of church discipline, but the same commitment to moral excellence and holiness required in the Old Testament is demanded in the New.

Anyone can see the kind of behaviour that belongs to the lower nature: fornication, impurity, and indecency; idolatry and sorcery; quarrels, a contentious temper, envy, fits of rage, selfish ambitions, dissensions, party intrigues, and jealousies; drinking bouts, orgies, and the like. I warn you, as I warned you before, that those who behave in such ways will never inherit the kingdom of God. (Galatians 5:19-21 NEB)

Make no mistake: no fornicator or idolater, none who are guilty either of adultery or of homosexual perversion, no thieves or grabbers or drunkards or slanderers or swindlers, will possess the kingdom of God. (1 Corinthians 6:9b-10 NEB)

Paul warned that none who practice the licentious, God-defying life styles of our time can enter into the Kingdom of God.

HOLINESS REQUIRES EFFORT

The alarming prevalence and destructiveness of AIDS and other sexually transmitted diseases should open our eyes to the monster we created when we set aside biblical standards. Because men and women constantly set aside these moral and spiritual principles, today's divorce rates are soaring. Such licentiousness demands strong resistance on our part.

As God's people, we are called to subdue these sensual lusts, to control the "lower nature" or the flesh. It requires effort on our part. Paul enjoins all believers:

This I say then, walk in the Spirit, and ye shall not fulfill the lust of the flesh. (Galatians 5:16)

But put ye on the Lord Jesus Christ, and make not provision for the flesh, to fulfil the lusts thereof. (Romans 13:14)

That, leaving your former way of life, you must lay aside that old human nature which, deluded by its lusts, is sinking towards death. You must be made new in mind and spirit, and put on the new nature of God's creating, which shows itself in the just and devout life called for by the truth. (Ephesians 4:22-24 NEB)

Unfortunately, despite such scriptural admonitions, Christians too become caught in the web of sexual sin.

One of the grievous sins of our degenerate age of corruption is "Adultery." But if the transgressor of the Seventh Commandment were to be found only among those who do not profess to be Christ's followers, the evil would not have been a tenth part as great as it now is. But the crime of adultery is largely committed by professed Christians. Both clergymen and laymen, whose names stand fair upon the church records, are alike guilty. Many who profess to be ministers of Christ are like the sons of Eli who ministered in the sacred office, but took advantage of their office to engage in crime and commit adultery.[2]

The immorality syndrome, which often results in divorce, has caught ministers as well as members. Homes of good men have been assaulted by this menace. There seems to be no exception—kings, peasants, leaders, high and low, rich and poor—all are exposed to this behavioral antagonist.

But why do Christians fall? One commentator said, "All should bear in mind that Satan's special efforts are directed against the ministry." But the news that follows that statement is undoubtedly good news. "Stringent policies now in force (in the church) make it impossible for a minister once found guilty of a violation of the Seventh Commandment, ever again to bear the sacred credentials."[3]

THE CALL

The call for purity and holiness is never more urgent. Both the Old and New Testament moral standards are impartial. The same law is for all and obedience to it is the key to marital happiness. Those who neglect to fully commit themselves to Christ and to the moral principles of His Word can never hope to withstand the licentiousness of this age.

The Lord made man upright, but he has fallen and become degraded, because he refused to yield obedience to the sacred claims which the law of God has upon him. All the passions of man, if properly controlled and rightly directed will contribute to his physical and moral health and ensure him a great amount of happiness. The adulterer, and fornicator and the incontinent do not enjoy life. There can be no true enjoyment for the transgressor of God's law. The Lord knew this, therefore he restricts man, he directs, commands, and he positively forbids.[4]

Dearly beloved, I beseech you as strangers and pilgrims, abstain from fleshly lusts which war against the soul. (1 Peter 2:11)

The devout life that truth calls for can be fully attained through the indwelling power of the Spirit of Christ who abides in the hearts and lives of believers. Will you allow the cleansing influence of the Spirit of Christ to work in you? It is the formula for lasting happiness at home; it is the surest way to avoid the humdrum and heartache of divorce and remarriage.

So, in conclusion, "I speak after the manner of men because of the infirmity of your flesh: for as ye have yielded your members servants to uncleanness and to iniquity unto iniquity; even so now yield your members servants to righteousness unto holiness. ... But now being made free from sin, and become servants of God, ye have your fruit unto holiness, and the end everlasting life" (Rom. 6:19;22). "The soul's interest should not be trifled with. Your capital is your character. There should not be one departure from reserve. Moral purity, self respect, and a strong resistance, are to be constantly cherished."[5]

Crucifying the flesh and walking after the Spirit in righteousness is the standard of the New Testament, and under no circumstances should God's people deviate from these lofty ideals which God has set forth.

NOTES AND REFERENCES

1. Riedel, Tracy, and Moskowitz, *The Book of the Bible*, 225.

2. Ellen G. White, *Marriage and Divorce* compiled by Leah Smitke, 70.

3. Ibid., 71.

4. *Review and Herald* (March 8, 1870).

5. White, *Marriage and Divorce*, 101.

Chapter 3

The Shammah-Hillel Dispute

Someone may ask, "What does divorce have to do with a man's salvation?" To some it does not really matter since salvation is not of works, but other, more pragmatic, Christians are concerned about the many and varied interpretations usually given to the biblical concept of divorce. They are concerned about the relationship of divorce to the total Christian experience. They want to know what the Bible teaches about the subject and what the will of God is in the matter of divorce and remarriage.

Crudence Concordance of the Bible defines divorce as "the legal dissolution of marriage." Moses tolerated divorce (Deut. 24:1-4). Later the rabbinical scholars Shammah and his disciple Hillel produced two schools of thought concerning divorce. The school of Shammah taught that a man could not be lawfully divorced from his wife unless he found her guilty of some action which was really infamous and contrary to the rules of virtue. But the school of Hillel taught that, on the contrary, the least reasons were sufficient to authorize a man to put away his wife: her bad cooking or his finding another woman whom he liked better. The Pharisees, knowing this, attempted to trap Jesus into some statement with which they could take issue. However, Jesus declined to interpret Moses' words, declaring only that He regarded all causes less than fornication as too weak of grounds for divorce.[1]

When comparing the teachings of these two rabbinical scholars, Shammah's teachings appear to conform closest to that of Christ's.

DIVORCE: A HUMAN TRAGEDY

Various dictionaries define divorce as "severance, separation, the legal dissolution of a marriage," etc. It means to end a marriage by law; to terminate a marriage contract by a means other than death. Divorce is that legal and binding dissolution of a marriage compact to which (sometimes) both parties may agree when they no longer desire to continue their union with each other. Divorce is a permanent action. It is different from what in some countries is known as "legal separation."

Legal separation (or *divortium imperfectum*) is a proviso that grants both spouses a cooling-off period during which their marital differences may be adjusted and their marriage, if possible, retrieved and revived. It indicates that both parties in a marriage have been temporarily separated by law, but for all practical purposes remain legally married and bound to each other by the conjugal covenant. So, "spouses who are legally separated may not remarry." Some jurisdictions have no provision for legal separation. Then there is no legal means of separation apart from divorce.[2]

Why So Many Divorces?

Why are there so many divorces in society today? Kistler says that "failure [of marriages] may be traced to personal difficulties that couples are unwilling or unable to solve."[3] He concludes that the most obvious answer to this question is that "there are more people in the nation [the USA] than ever before, resulting in more marriages and thus in the possibility of more failed marriages."

We must not forget, however, that some changes taking place in our society have influenced our social order. Bowman and Spanner, renowned sociologists, suggest the following social factors as contributing to the high divorce rate:

1. Decreased tolerance of poor marital quality.

2. Higher status of women.

3. New standards of marital success.

4. New ideals of married life.

5. Decline of religious authority.

6. Greater liberalism of thought.

7. Changed ideas about masculine supremacy.

8. Increased urbanization.

9. Increased ability of women to support themselves if they get divorced.

10. Greater ease with which a divorce may be obtained.

11. More widespread acceptance of divorce.

12. A breakdown of family control.

13. A more tolerant attitude toward those who are divorced.[4]

Two contributors to *World Book Encyclopedia*, Brigette M. Bodenheimer, professor of law at the University of California at Davis, and William M. Kemphart, professor of sociology at the University of Pennsylvania, present the following reasons for higher divorce rates: "Most men and women who seek a divorce, do so because they cannot solve certain problems in their marriages. Such problems may include difference in goals, financial difficulties, or poor sexual relationships."[5] Many local situations also contribute to divorce, but generally, wise people will learn how to cope with personal differences and give their marriage a chance to work.

A Background of Divorce

Volume 4 of the *New Catholic Encyclopedia* gives the following perspective of divorce in primitive societies:

> Although all known primitive societies endorse the value of stable marriages, only a few societies do not permit divorce under some circumstances. Among those that allow it, about three fourths do not specify conditions and grounds. The parties to a marriage (or less frequently, only the men) are permitted to divorce for their own reasons.

> Among the groups that specify grounds, adultery and inability to bear children are frequently stipulated as just cause for divorce. Laziness, suspected witchcraft, failure to cook properly, bad temper, and neglectfulness, are among the many other specific complaints some times accepted as grounds.[6]

The Babylonians

"In ancient Babylon, the code of Hammurabi imposed certain specified monetary settlements upon a man who divorced his wife, and allowed a woman also to initiate divorce, in which case her husband could divorce her without alimony."[7]

The Arabians

"The customary rights of the husband was not restricted among the Arabians until the time of Mohammed (570-632). Neither the Jews nor the Arabs recognized women's rights to divorce, although under certain circumstances, a wife could bring suit for dissolution of her marriage."[8]

The Peoples of India

"In ancient India, although divorce was common among the Dravidian and Tibeto-Burma tribes, the Hindus accepted marriage as normally monogamic and indissoluble, until death, except on occasions of abandonment of a faithful wife, adultery of the wife, or serious offenses against a husband."[9]

The Greeks and Romans

"Both the Greeks and Romans had traditions of great marital stability in their early periods. Divorce later became easy and common, however, so that in Athens a man could divorce his wife merely by giving notice; a man and his wife might dissolve their marriage by mutual consent, or a wife might appeal to the archon for divorce on recognized grounds (which do not include adultery of the husband). Divorce was a purely private matter, first for the husband, eventually for either party. By the 2nd century B.C. divorce was common in the most prominent social circles, and by the time of Cicero (106-143 B.C.) it was fashionable."[10]

The United States Today

"Divorce is a sizable problem in the United States, and many other countries. Experts estimate that about 35 percent of all U.S. marriages end in divorce. In more than half of these divorces, the couple has children under 18 years of age. Divorce rarely occurred in the American colonies. Some colonies made no provision for divorce at all. But by the mid 1800's almost every state had a divorce law. Today, the U.S. divorce rate is about 16 times as high as it was in 1867, the first year for which the Bureau of the Census published divorce figures."[11]

Among the Hebrew Patriarchs

Jewish divorce first became legal in the time of Moses. There is apparently no evidence of men legally separating from their wives or women from their husbands before this period. Two of the most oft-quoted successful marriages of the Bible, that of Abraham and Sarah and of Isaac and Rebecca, predates the time of Moses. Although these two homes experienced their share of marital difficulties, and were at times almost overwhelmed by depression and despair, neither husband nor wife attempted to divorce or abandon each other. Abraham did not divorce Sarah because she was barren, neither did Sarah divorce Abraham because of his sexual involvement with her maid Hagar, perplexing as this was to the peace and tranquility of the family (Gen. 16:1-4). Isaac did not divorce Rebecca for colluding with their son Jacob in the scheme to deceive him and deprive their other son Esau of his birthright (Gen. 27:1-17). Such fraud would have been sufficient grounds for a divorce in some courts today. Laban's first daughter, Leah, was deceitfully thrust upon the youthful Jacob, yet Jacob did not consider divorcing his unsolicited wife, Leah (Gen. 29:21-25). Neither did Moses divorce his Cushite wife because his family and friends rejected her (Num. 12:1).

Unlike in our day when almost 50 percent of those who enter marriage eventually divorce or separate, the "quickie divorce" was unheard of in patriarchal times.

THE DEUTORONOMIC LAW

During Moses' time the Hebrews became a great people of national status. The need for laws to mediate and regulate family disturbances became acute. As the people multiplied in numbers, so did their social problems. Although marriage was largely a private affair, marital problems were destined to become community and state problems. Naturally some legal instrument had to be invented to deal with this new emergency. It was probably during this time that Moses, the servant of God, introduced his famous divorce bill which is so widely used in our day. His divorce legislation was clearly intended to spare the nation's families much of the anguish and bitterness that resulted from confrontations between warring spouses. The precise intent of the bill is clearly stated in the law itself: "and *thou shalt not cause the land to sin* which the LORD thy God giveth thee for an inheritance" (Deut. 24:4b).

We may draw our own conclusions about the morality or immorality of divorce, but it is difficult to conceive of a sinful society operating without such a provision. The Deuteronomic law was the divorce instrument used for centuries up until the time of Christ. It was to this law that the Savior referred in His various discussions on divorce and remarriage. As one examines Christ's references to Moses' law, two very important conclusions emerge. First, it was not God's intention that marriage be treated in an *ad hoc* fashion as we do today, or that the sacred flames of the holy institution of wedlock should go out through ignorance or misinformation. Second, divorce was primarily an emergency provision, to be applied only in exceptional cases and with much care and compassion.

Some believe that Moses yielded to the people out of weakness and wrote this law, but nothing could be further from the truth.

Moses: An Authority

Moses was one of the most inspired authorities and writers of the Bible. His actions were, with few exceptions, generally approved by God.

And Moses said, Hereby ye shall know that the LORD hath sent me to do all these works; for I have not done them of mine own mind. (Numbers 16:28)

And the LORD came down in the pillar of the cloud and stood in the door of the taber-nacle...and He said, Hear now My words...My servant Moses is...faithful in all Mine house. With him will I speak, mouth to mouth...the LORD shall he behold: wherefore then were ye not afraid to speak against My servant Moses? (Numbers 12:5-8)

The Scriptures describe Moses as "very meek, above all the men which were upon the face of the earth" (Num. 12:3). But he certainly was not the weakest man. Meekness is not necessarily weak-ness. The character of this great servant of God is best judged by his response to circumstances that demanded firmness and decision. When Moses spot-ted an Egyptian assaulting his fellow Hebrew, he quickly destroyed the Egyptian (Num. 2:11-12). Such a display of patriotism bears no resemblance to cow-ardice or capitulation. That action was not one of a weak-kneed soldier.

Moses was able to make tough decisions and tough choices. He exhibited a rare blend of compas-sion and realism, of humility and sternness, as seen in no other of his peers. He was a distinguished leader with a strong and stable personality. Even in the New Testament he is described as "faithful in all his house" (Heb. 3:2).

Jesus confirmed the authority of Moses as well.

And he said unto him, If they hear not Moses and the prophets, neither will they be persuaded though one rose from the dead. (Luke 16:31)

For had ye believed Moses, ye would have believed Me: for he wrote of Me. But if ye believe not his writings, how shall ye believe My words? (John 5:46-47)

Moses' divorce law was no reflection of weakness on his part. It was more than a social instrument; it was to have far-reaching consequences. According to Deuteronomy, the law was to be a defense against sin. Designed to help stem the growing tide of iniquity in the nation, it was drawn up apparently with God's glory in mind. This legislation obviously had a spiritual purpose and a divine authorization, a fact which should not be overlooked when studying divorce and remarriage from the biblical perspective.

The Law As It Was Written

Here is the law as it was given by Moses in Deuteronomy.

When a man hath taken a wife, and married her, and it come to pass that she find no favour

*in his eyes, because he hath found **some un-cleanness** in her: then let him write her a bill of divorcement, and give it in her hand, and send her out of his house. And when she is departed out of his house, she may go and be another man's wife. And if the latter husband hate her, and write her a bill of divorcement, and giveth it in her hand, and sendeth her out of his house; or if the latter husband die, which took her to be his wife; her former husband, which sent her away, may not take her again to be his wife, after that she is defiled....*
(Deuteronomy 24:1-4)

Here is the same passage in another version.

If a man doesn't like something about his wife, he may write a letter stating that he has divorced her, give her the letter, and send her away. If she then remarries, and the second husband also divorces her, or dies, the former husband may not marry her again, for she has been defiled.... (Deuteronomy 24:1-4 TLB)

The Bill of Divorcement

Although other nations permitted oral divorce, Jewish laws required written documentation: "...let him write her a *bill of divorcement,* and give it in her hand..." (Deut. 24:1). It would be interesting to see an original copy of this ancient document, the bill of divorcement. What was it like?

Dr. Edersheim said that "the bill was couched in explicit terms."[12] The bill was defined with such clarity and precision that even the river nearest the home of the divorcing parties was specified. This document was so important that it was considered invalid if prepared in a gentile court. Why was the bill to be so clear and unambiguous? *The Expositor's Greek Testament* answers this question in the following words: "They were zealous to have the bill in due form that the woman might be able to show she was free to marry again."[13]

The famous Rabbi Maimonides and other Jewish sources recorded this ancient document in the 12th century. The following is a translated copy of the original divorce bill as taken from Jewish Encyclopedias.[14]

On this _____ day of the week...day of the month...in the year...I, who am also called son of...of the city of...by the river of...do hereby consent with my own will, being under no restraint, and I do hereby release, send away, and put aside thee, my wife...who is also called daughter of...who is this day in the city of...by the river of...who have been my wife for some time past! and thus I do release thee, and send thee away and put thee aside that thou mayest have permission and control over thyself to go to be married to any man that thou mayest desire; and that no man shall hinder thee from this day forward, and thou art permitted to any man, and this shall be unto thee from me, a bill of dismissal, a document of release, and a letter of freedom, according to the law of Moses and Israel.

_____ The Son of _____ Witness

_____ The Son of _____ Witness

"The bill or writing of divorcement implied not only a mere separation from bed and board as some restrict it, but a complete severance of the marriage tie."[15] Notice also that there is no attempt to discredit the guilty one or to give reasons for the breakup in this bill.

EXAMINING THE LAW

Moses' divorce bill was open to much exploitation: A man could divorce his wife for every cause. If he liked another woman better than his wife, then if he wished, he could divorce her and marry the woman of his choice. Naturally a bill of this draft had serious imperfections. Controversy was unavoidable. Christ at once closed the gaps in the law by permitting divorce only on one ground: *fornication.* "And I say unto you, Whosoever shall put away his wife, except it be for *fornication,* and shall marry another, committeth adultery..." (Mt. 19:9). Fornication is sometimes described as sexual immorality, infidelity, or unfaithfulness to the marriage vows.

The Grounds for Divorce

Moses' law differs from Christ's on a number of points. The Deuteronomic law allowed divorce for non-moral offenses. If a husband did not like his wife's responses, he could divorce her. Divorce could be pursued for simple misdemeanors. But according to Christ, a divorce is lawful only on grounds of immorality. It must be a proven case of unchastity or sexual sin. Adultery must be involved. Moses' law stipulated the death penalty for adultery (see Lev. 20:10). An adulterous spouse, when found guilty of the crime, was generally stoned. In that case the marriage was dissolved by death instead of by divorce. In such instances there was no problem with the innocent party remarrying after the execution of the unfaithful spouse. The marriage covenant vanished at death, in accordance with the law of marriage which prevailed even up until the time of the apostles: "For the woman which hath an husband is bound by the law to her husband so long as he liveth; but if the husband be dead, she is loosed from the law of her husband" (Rom. 7:2).

But Christ outlawed this punishment (Jn. 8:5) and instead allowed divorce for adultery (Mt. 19:9). Divorce for adultery was unheard of in Moses' time. The divorce for fornication priviso was introduced by Christ, and from there on superceded Moses' law. Under the Deuteronomic law, the guilty spouse was silenced. She was no longer responsible for the future of her marriage. That became the responsibility of the innocent mate, who nearly always was the husband. It was his option to pardon and forgive his guilty wife, and thereby preserve their marriage, or to make her a public scandal by putting her out of his house (which is a classic example of harshness and hardness of heart; see Mt. 19:8).

Guy Duty in quoting the Talmud and Josephus, said in effect that In Moses' time as in other times, many Jews were cruel to their wives and because of their cruelty and hardness of heart, God permitted divorce. These cruel Jews divorced their wives for every cause. They divorced them for the most frivolous reasons. If she burned his biscuits, or didn't season his food right, or if he did not like her manners or if she was a poor housekeeper, even if he finds a woman more handsome than her. Repudiation of her marriage at his whim and pleasure was at the heart of Jewish divorce legislation.[16]

At the same time, it apparently was not necessary to stone everyone found guilty of adultery as the law required. Privy divorce was an alternative. It was, in some sense, an extension of grace to the offender. It allowed a man to divorce his wife privately, even for immorality, without the trauma of a public trial before Jewish tribunals. Such a practice hindered scandal and the risk of a guilty wife being put to death by stoning.[17]

Not many examples of privy divorce are in the Bible. It does not appear to have been very common in Bible times. One of the clearest examples, however, of privy divorce is recorded in Matthew 1:19: "Then Joseph her husband, being a just man, and not willing to make her a publick example, was minded to put her away [divorce her] privily." Joseph apparently intended to use this divorce instrument to put away his betrothed wife, Mary, for adultery. Persons who violated their betrothal vows were given the same penalties as those who violated their marriage vows (see Deut. 22:22-29).

What Is Uncleanness?

The original divorce statute rested on the premise that it was the husband who had found some uncleanness in his wife (Deut. 24:1). "Some Hebrew grammarians have been uncertain about the meaning of 'uncleanness' here. The Hebrew term is *ervah-dover*, and it had various interpretations in the Jewish *Talmud* in different centuries and in various countries. It is translated 'obnoxious' and 'unseemly' in the Jewish *Torah* and *Masoretic Text*."[18]

"Dr. Alfred Edersheim said this uncleanness 'included every kind of impropriety, such as going about with loose hair, spinning in the street, familiarily talking with men, ill-treating her husband's parents in his presence, brawling, that is, "speaking to her husband so loudly that the neighbors could hear her

in the adjoining house" (*Chetuband* vii 6), a general
bad reputation, or the discovery of fraud before marriage.' "[19] Guy Duty says, "Some argue that this
uncleanness was immorality, but this could not be
true because the unfaithful Jewess was stoned to
death."[20]

Various modern translations use different words
for "uncleanness" in Deuteronomy 24:1. For example, the New American Standard Bible uses "indecency." The Living Bible translates "uncleanness" as
"something he does not like." The New World Translation speaks of "something indecent." The Revised
Standard Version also uses a similar expression: "because he has found some indecency in her."

Dr. Adam Clarke comments:

Some uncleanness, means *any cause of dislike*. It
is certain that a Jew may put away his wife for
any cause that seemed good to himself, and so
hard were their hearts that Moses suffered this,
and we find they continued this practice even to
the time of our Lord who strongly reprehended
them on the account, and showed that such
license was wholly inconsistent with the original
design of marriage.[21]

An inequity of this law is its assumption that the
wife is the one who always does something wrong, something worthy of divorce. This is not necessarily the
case, particularly in our day. The law grants husbands

the right to put away their wives, but makes no mention of wives putting away their husbands.

So in order to divorce his wife all a Jew had to do was give her the divorce bill in the presence of two witness. Thus the marriage was legally dissolved. This discharge from the house was all that was necessary to divorce a mate. Both were now free to remarry if they chose.

The Remarriage Issue

In western society, the number of times a person may be married and divorced is virtually limitless. (Actress Elizabeth Taylor has been married nine times.) A man may be married as many times as he pleases, if his culture, his religion, and his country allow it.

Moses' bill allowed remarriage after a divorce: "And when she is departed out of his house, she may go and be another man's wife" (Deut. 24:2). With a bill of divorcement in her hands, a guilty wife could seek remarriage without difficulty.

The Deuteronomic law also says, "Her former husband, which sent her away, may not take her again to be his wife, after that she is defiled..." (Deut. 24:4). I am a bit curious why it does not say "former husbands" (plural). Would that not have signified her liberty to marry several husbands? Instead the law prohibited a divorcée from returning to her "former husband" (one only, not several). The evidence seems conclusive that being twice married and twice divorced, the record was closed to any further marriages for the divorcée. Such a conclusion is further substantiated by the fact that such a spouse was to be considered "defiled" (Deut. 24:4). Even under that loose system of easy divorce the law did not allow remarriage for a woman with more than two husbands alive (though she was married only to one; the first is called a "former husband").

Opponents of this view argue that the wording of the text simply restricted the divorcée from returning to her "former husband," but left her free to remarry as many times as she pleased. This argument is unwarranted. It is reading into the passage an unfounded opinion. There was no need to rule beyond two husbands since the law clearly stated that after the second marriage "she is defiled." Another marriage would therefore be an "abomination before the LORD" (Deut. 24:4). In Christ's day, however, the situation had deteriorated to the point where women were known to have been married as many as four, five, or even six, times (see Jn. 4:16-18).

Christ's teaching on this issue was somewhat different from that of Moses. Jesus taught that "whosoever shall put away his wife, except it be for fornication, *and shall marry another*, committeth adultery: and *whoso marrieth her* which is put away *doth commit adultery*" (Mt. 19:9). Under Christ, remarriage becomes a more sensitive issue, since according to Him adultery might be committed in the venture.

Dr. Adam Clarke's comments on the phrase of Deuteronomy, "she is defiled," follow that same line of thought:

> Does not this refer to her having been divorced and married in consequence to another? Though God, for the hardness of their hearts, suffered them to put away their wives, yet he considered all after marriages, in that case to be pollution and defilement. It is on this ground that our Lord argues that whoever marries the woman that is put away is an adulterer. Now this could not have been the case, if God had allowed the divorce to be a legal and proper separation of the man from his wife, but in the sight of God, nothing can be a legal cause of separation but adultery on either side. In such a case, a man may put away his wife and a wife may put away her husband.[22]

According to Dr. Clarke's theology, an attempt to divorce a spouse for any cause other than adultery is unlawful. Therefore the marriage covenant may still be binding in spite of the divorce. Consequently, a person who comes along and marries a divorcee may be involving him or herself in a legal entanglement with a marriage that, although out of function, may still be in force and valid. Thus the spouse would be committing adultery. Robert Kistler touches on this issue:

> "Societies'" courts may release a person from an unhappy marriage, but marriage is more than a legal contract. At marriage, vows were taken in the sight of God as well, and no court in the land can presume to act for God in releasing a couple from such vows. Thus, a legally divorced person may commit adultery as far as the church is concerned in entering a second marriage.[23]

Ellen G. White supports this viewpoint.

> A woman may be legally divorced from her husband by the laws of the land and yet not divorced in the sight of God, and according to the higher law. There is only one sin which is adultery, which can place the husband or wife in a position where they can be free from the marriage vow in the sight of God. Although the laws of the land may grant a divorce, yet they are husband and wife still, in the Bible light, according to the laws of God.[24]

THE AUTHORITY TO DIVORCE

The following are six known sources and laws from which the authority to divorce and remarry is usually drawn:

1. Moses' divorce law (Deut. 24:1-4).

2. Christ's teachings on divorce (Mt. 5:32; 19:3-9).

3. Paul's marriage law (1 Cor. 7:1-16).

4. Writings and practices of church fathers.

5. Laws of the various states and governments.

6. Rules and culture of different religions.

The authority to divorce and remarry usually comes from one of these sources. All the religions of the world possess their own peculiar concepts and values which they apply to divorce and remarriage. Moslems, Jews, Fundamentalists, Baptists, Jehovah's Witnesses, and others all cherish differing concepts and views on this subject. However, each personifies either the Shammah or the Hillel viewpoint of marriage. Some allow divorce; others do not permit any divorce for whatever reason.

The true biblical position on divorce and remarriage should be known. It is imperative that the Word of God be the counsellor on all these issues. To do otherwise is to court disaster. Moral depravity is excess baggage for the Christian who is called upon to lay aside every weight and sin that so easily trips him or her up. Christians are called to run with patience the race that is set before them and to walk worthily before God (Heb. 12:1). Naturally, the civil laws of state are to be respected and obeyed. God has ordained them and no Christian has the right to willfully disregard or flaunt the laws of state (1 Pet. 2:13-16). But when state laws contradict, or come into conflict with the moral laws of God, when a wedding is to be decided on the basis of one of these laws, either the law of state or the law of God, then each of us must decide to "obey God rather than men" (Acts 5:29).

For the Christian, the spiritual laws of God must take pre-eminence over the laws and customs of men, particularly in matters of divorce and remarriage. Would that all Christians understand that before they proceed to divorce only on purely legal grounds (that is, on the basis of the laws of state only). A marriage authorized by the state and not by the Word of God may be unlawful, placing the mate's spiritual life in jeopardy.

NOTES AND REFERENCES

1. *Crudence Concordance*, 154.

2. *World Book Encyclopedia* Vol. 5, 210A.

3. Robert C. Kistler, *Marriage, Divorce, and...*, (Review and Herald Publ. Assoc.), 124.

4. Bowman and Spanner, *Modern Marriage*, 148-149.

5. *World Book Encyclopedia* Vol. 5, 210A.

6. *New Catholic Encyclopedia* (1967) Vol. 4, 928.

7. Ibid.

8. Ibid.

9. Ibid.

10. Ibid.

11. *World Book Encyclopedia* Vol. 5, 210A.

12. *Sketches of Jewish Life*, 158.

13. *The Expositor's Greek Testament* Vol. 1, 109.

14. Guy Duty, *Divorce and Remarriage*, (Bethany House Publ.), 35.

15. Pulpit Commentary—Mark v. 2 p. 95 (old edition); as quoted by Duty, *Divorce and Remarriage*, 34-35.

16. *Talmud* Gittin 9.10; *Josephus*, 134; as quoted in Duty, *Divorce and Remarraige*, 21-22.

17. Duty, *Divorce and Remarriage* (Bethany House Publ.).

18. Jewish Pub. Society, 1962, as quoted in Duty, *Divorce and Remarriage*, 22.

19. Alfred Edersheim, *Skethes of Jewish Social Life*, (Erdmans Pub. Co., 1957), 157-158; as quoted in Duty, *Divorce and Remarriage*, 23.

20. Duty, *Divorce and Remarriage*, 22-23.

21. *Clarke's Commentary*, 221.

22. *Clarke's Commentary*, 221.

23. Kistler, *Marriage, Divorce, and...*, 124.

24. Ellen G. White, *Adventist Home*, 344.

Chapter 4

What Jesus Taught About Divorce

Jesus is the supreme Authority on divorce and remarriage. Not only is He an authority on the subject, He is also the Author and Producer of the great moral law of God, including the law of marriage. Who is more capable of answering questions regarding interpretations, obligations, and requirements of the law than the Law Giver Himself? (Jas. 4:12) His teachings on divorce and remarriage should be considered final.

The depth of Jesus' teachings on divorce and remarriage vary between the three synoptic Gospels.

However, the differences are of little significance, so long as the Master's message remains clear, unambiguous and without distortion or departure from the truth as He taught it. One thing appears to be certain. Whether Christ routinely expounded the law or simply answered the Pharisees' queries, His teachings were always authoritative, clear and unequivocal. Misinterpretations were not possible, for His doctrines were without discrepancy.

Jesus constantly addressed family issues. In the Sermon on the Mount, for instance, He dealt with the issue of divorce and remarriage long before the Pharisees raised the question. He pointed to immorality as the most serious threat to family stability and happiness. According to Him, obedience to the commandments of God is the only proper way to sanctify and preserve a marriage. However, His most scathing deliberations on the subject were triggered by a question from a contingent of Pharisees. They came to Him not to learn about truth or to understand God's will for their lives, but to trap Him into some cunningly contrived argument that they could use to accuse Him of contempt of Moses' law. Such a felony provoked serious consequences in rabbinical courts.

A LOOK AT THE ISSUE

The Pharisees came to Jesus with a sneaky question: "Is it lawful for a man to put away his wife for every cause?" (Mt. 19:3b)

Some argue that the Pharisees had come mainly to solicit Christ's views on the Shammah-Hillel dispute over the legitimate causes for divorce, but nothing can be further from the truth. The Pharisees had ulterior motives. Besides, Jesus' insistence on purity and holiness of heart in His replies shows that He was not acting as referee between the two giants, Shammah and Hillel, in their dispute over legitimate grounds for divorce. His mission was not one of a mediator or arbitrator of local disputes. (See Luke 12:13-14.)

Jesus did not enter into any controversy with the scheming Pharisees. He very wisely treated the institution of divorce as one which should not have occurred in the first place, saying, "...from the beginning it was not so" (Mt. 19:8).

Neither did Jesus make any attempt to abolish the divorce law of Moses (Deut. 24:1-4), or to introduce any new bill. Instead He held rather closely to Moses' original law and its purpose. Christ gave added luster and meaning to this law, while at the same time He publicly recognized the abuse and exploitation to which the Jewish leaders and people often subjected it. He accepted the validity of divorce and went on record as supporting it under certain conditions. But it was the spiritual aspect of divorce that most occupied the Master's attention, and not so much its social or economic consequences.

Obedience to the commandments of God was at the heart of all of His divorce deliberations.

REVIEWING THE ACCOUNTS

Christ's remarks on divorce and remarriage are recorded in the synoptic Gospels—Matthew, Mark, and Luke. Mark's Gospel records Christ's discussions of divorce and remarriage in 11 verses (Mk. 10:2-12). Matthew's record spreads it over a total of 16 verses (Mt. 5:27-32; 19:3-12). But Luke compresses it all into one solitary verse: "Whosoever putteth away his wife, and marrieth another, committeth adultery: and whosoever marrieth her that is put away from her husband committeth adultery" (Lk. 16:18).

The version in Mark's Gospel is not quite as extensive as Matthew's. Obviously, Mark omits some of the details given by Matthew, but adds a few of his own.

And the Pharisees came to Him, and asked Him, Is it lawful for a man to put away his wife? tempting Him. And He answered and said unto them, What did Moses command you? And they said, Moses suffered to write a bill of divorcement, and to put her away. And Jesus answered and said unto them, For the hardness of your heart he wrote you this precept. But from the beginning of the creation God made them male and female. For this

*cause shall a man leave his father and mother,
and cleave to his wife; and they twain [two]
shall be one flesh: so then they are no more
twain, but one flesh. What therefore God hath
joined together, let not man put asunder. ... And
He saith unto them, Whosoever shall put away
his wife, and marry another, committeth adultery against her. And if a woman shall put
away her husband, and be married to another,
she committeth adultery. (Mark 10:2-9;11-12)*

Matthew records Christ's conversations on marriage and divorce in two different places: Matthew
5:27-32 and Matthew 19:3-12. First is the account in
the fifth chapter, which is usually referred to as the
Sermon on the Mount. So Christ had addressed the
divorce-remarriage issue long before the Pharisees
came to Him with their conniving question about
causes for divorce. Christ's interest in the subject
was not an afterthought. He had dealt with the matter some time before. For God understands all of
men's problems and provided for their resolution in
Christ, even before the actual situation arose.

*Ye have heard that it was said by them of old
time, Thou shalt not commit adultery: but I say
unto you, That whosoever looketh on a woman
to lust after her hath committed adultery with
her already in his heart. And if thy right eye offend thee, pluck it out, and cast it from thee: for
it is profitable for thee that one of thy members*

should perish, and not that thy whole body should be cast into hell. ... It hath been said, Whosoever shall put away his wife, let him give her a writing of divorcement: but I say unto you, That whosoever shall put away his wife, saving for the cause of fornication, causeth her to commit adultery: and whosoever shall marry her that is divorced committeth adultery. (Matthew 5:27-29;31-32)

*The Pharisees also came unto Him, tempting Him, and saying unto Him, Is it lawful for a man to put away his wife for every cause? And He answered and said unto them, Have ye not read, that He which made them at the beginning made them male and female, and said, For this cause shall a man leave father and mother, and shall cleave to his wife: and they twain shall be one flesh? Wherefore they are no more twain, but one flesh. What therefore God hath joined together, let not man put asunder. They say unto Him, Why did Moses then command to give a writing of divorcement, and to put her away? He saith unto them, Moses because of the hardness of your hearts suffered you to put away your wives: but from the beginning it was not so. And I say unto you, Whosoever shall put away his wife, **except it be for fornication**, and shall marry another, committeth adultery: and whoso marrieth her which* *is put away **doth** commit adultery. His disciples say unto Him, If the case of the man be so with his wife, it is not good to marry. But He said unto them, All men cannot receive this saying, save they to whom it is given. For there are some eunuchs, which were so born from their mother's womb: and there are some eunuchs, which were made eunuchs of men: and there be eunuchs, which have made themselves eunuchs for the kingdom of heaven's sake. He that is able to receive it, let him receive it.* (Matthew 19:3-12)

Matthew's report is the most comprehensive of all. Only in Matthew's Gospel is there any mention of an "exception for the cause of fornication" (Mt. 5:32; 19:9). That phrase does not appear in any of the other Gospels. Mark and Luke make no mention of such an exception.

DIVORCE—RULE OR EXCEPTION

"And I say unto you, Whosoever shall put away his wife, *except* it be for fornication, and shall marry another, committeth adultery..." (Mt. 19:9). Jesus did not say that there was to be no divorce at all, but He made divorce an exception rather than a rule. According to Jesus, divorce is an anomaly, an invader of the human family. God never ordained divorce; He simply permitted it because of the hardness of men's hearts. It was not in His plan that men should ever separate from their wives or women from their husbands. Marriage was to be indissoluble. A man may repudiate his wife and marry another woman only for the cause of fornication.

Although Jesus did not extol divorce as a way of life for any, He knew very well that without such a provision, the temptation to escape from bankrupt marriages through violent or unethical means would be great. Such a situation could create a crisis for the Church and for society in general. He, therefore, made divorce an exception. Divorce alone may avert some crises that refuse to be controlled by other means, but divorce was to be viewed only as an exception for fornication, and not as a rule.

People often revert to this exception clause in Matthew 19:9 as their stronghold (except for the cause of fornication). They discover in this legislation the ideal route by which they may escape their embattled marriages with as little criticism as possible. They find in it a convenient club with which they may subdue all who disagree with their marriage and remarriage habits. It is inconceivable but true that some spouses even stoop so low as to wish that their mates would fall into temptation and commit adultery, since such an advantage would ease the pressure and allow them to divorce and remarry with a quieted conscience. They take advantage of

Christ's exception of divorce for fornication. But they overlook one important fact: Christ's divorce legislation included a rule as well as an exception.

In the plainest terms Jesus repeated the rule and then gave the exception. Here is the rule: "He saith unto them, Moses because of the hardness of your hearts suffered you to put away your wives: but from the beginning it was not so" (Mt. 19:8); "And said, For this cause shall a man leave father and mother, and shall cleave to his wife: and they twain shall be one flesh" (Mt. 19:5); "...What therefore God hath joined together, let not man put asunder" (Mt. 19:6).

The apostle Paul reiterated this same rule several years later: "And unto the married I command, yet not I, but the Lord, Let not the wife depart from her husband: But and if she depart, let her remain unmarried, or be reconciled to her husband: and let not the husband put away his wife" (1 Cor. 7:10-11); "For the woman which hath an husband is bound by the law to her husband so long as he liveth..." (Rom. 7:2).

This was God's rule in the beginning and there was to be no departure from it. No divorce crisis was to mar the homes of God's people, to separate wives from their husbands and children from their parents. Men and women united in the holy estate of matrimony were to love and cherish each other till death parted them.

Christ discussed both the rule and the exception, but He placed emphasis on the rule and not on the exception. The rule, according to Him, is permanence in marriage (Mt. 19:6) just as the marriage vows indicate: "till death do us part." Only by death are the nuptial bonds to be broken. When a marriage takes place, it ought to be a permanent affair. This is God's rule, according to Christ, but divorce for fornication is an exception to which He condescends because of the hardness of man's heart.

CHRIST'S SILENCE ON REMARRIAGE

Christ's statements on divorce also clearly indicate that He viewed remarriage after divorce as a foregone conclusion: "Anyone who divorces his wife and *marries another woman* commits adultery" (Lk. 16:18 NIV). It is presumed that the divorced husband remarries. In fact, what would be the purpose of pursuing a divorce if there was no option of remarrying another? But Christ's silence on the question of remarriage after divorce is puzzling.

Why were there no comments, parables, or instructions of any kind from the Savior's lips regarding remarriage? Could it be that His silence spoke louder than His words? Was what He did not say of more significance than what He had already said?

Silence is often more potent than the spoken word. Silence was one of the very persuasive means

Jesus used to convince His enemies that He was indeed the Son of God.

*And when He was accused of the chief priests and elders, He **answered nothing**. Then said Pilate unto Him, Hearest thou not how many things they witness against Thee? And He answered him to never a word; insomuch that the governor marvelled greatly.* (Matthew 27:12-14)

What lesson then was Jesus trying to teach us by His silence on the remarriage issue? Could it be that we ought to think much of the spiritual implications of divorce before becoming involved? A writer on divorce once asked, "Is not the silence of scripture on any subject significant? Where scripture is silent, should we not also be?"[1] Where Scripture is silent, who can speak with any certainty? Where the Master is silent, who else may speak with authority? Could Christ's silence on remarriage be taken to mean that remarriage after divorce may place the adherents on a spiritually uncertain path? We need to consider this carefully.

DIVORCE AND ADULTERY

Christ's main concern was that the sin of adultery might be committed in the remarriage shuffle. He believed that adultery began in the heart, that the adulterous thought and feeling precedes the adulterous act and life style (see Mt. 5:28). According to

Christ, adultery is surrendering to lustful passions through the lustful eye. It is sexual depravity, making unlawful sexual passes at others. Sexual activity within marriage is perfectly normal and proper. It is not sinful. "Marriage is honourable in all, and the bed undefiled" (Heb. 13:4). But the act becomes sinful when the union in which it is consummated is itself sinful: According to Christ, those entangled in unlawful marriage alliances, though legally married, are committing adultery.

I am told that the Greek background to the phrase "committeth adultery" in Luke 16:18 implies a continuous situation. The one who enters into an unlawful covenant has not only committed adultery once, but is living in a continuous state of adultery.

And He saith unto them, Whosoever shall put away his wife, and marry another, committeth adultery against her. (Mark 10:11; see also Luke 16:18)

Christ's teachings on divorce and its relationship to adultery is explicit enough. Putting away a spouse merely to make room for another who might be more exotic and acceptable, perhaps a former fiancé, a schoolmate, or some other person, is adultery. It is an invitation for the separated spouse to find companionship elsewhere, perhaps to even forge an adulterous alliance. Naturally a husband deserting or divorcing his wife may be the cause of the distraught woman becoming attached to some other man, thus taking the adulterous route. Can such a husband then in good conscience lay any claim to innocence? Under these circumstances can there be an innocent party? Are not both guilty of the sin of adultery? Even if the husband who put away his wife decides to remain chaste and not marry any other woman, he has already committed adultery by putting away his wife. Christ's reasoning here is clear and simple. Dissolving a marriage for causes other than unchastity is tantamount to adultery.

> But I tell you that anyone who divorces his wife, except for marital unfaithfulness, causes her to become an adulteress, and anyone who marries the divorced woman commits adultery. (Matthew 5:32 NIV)

> ...whosoever marrieth her that is put away from her husband committeth adultery. (Luke 16:18)

> Anyone who divorces his wife and marries another woman commits adultery, and **the man who marries a divorced woman commits adultery.** (Luke 16:18 NIV)

Moses' law allowed a divorced woman to go out and be another man's wife with only one restriction: On the death or default of her second husband, she was not to return to her former husband (see Deut. 24:1-4). But Christ clearly showed that marrying a divorcee increases the risk of becoming involved in a life-long adulterous partnership, which can cast a shadow across a believer's path for years to come. Such marriages often result in torture and torment to an otherwise guiltless conscience. Is it any wonder then that Jewish priests were forbidden to marry divorcees? (See Leviticus 21:14.) Nothing as uncertain as divorce was to be on the conscience of a minister of the sanctuary.

THEN WHY DIVORCE?

The Pharisees apparently were not satisfied with Christ's response to their first question, so they continued to probe: "They say unto Him, Why did Moses then command to give a writing of divorcement, and to put her away?" (Mt. 19:7)

Jesus replied without quibbling: "He saith unto them, Moses because of the hardness of your hearts suffered you to put away your wives: but from the beginning it was not so" (Mt. 19:8).

Hard-hearted men and women caused divorce. Its legislation was essential in order to cope with the moral and social ills that plagued the Israelite nation and the world. Yet the divorce bill was not to be administered without discretion; perhaps only when mediation and forgiveness had utterly failed. Such a law was probably necessary in order to minimize the risk of persons using violent and unlawful means of ending their unwanted marriages.

The Savior did not seek to sensationalize divorce or to overlook its tragic consequences, but His teachings made the divorce law an instrument of compassion rather than a tool of oppression, which the Israelites had done.

JESUS DID NOT SAY...

- That adultery is the unpardonable sin and that forgiveness is impossible once this sin has been committed.

- What actions the Church should take, if any, against those who transgress in the matter of divorce and remarriage.

- What a divorced spouse may do to regain control of him or herself after a divorce.

- What part the state was to play and the depth of its involvement in marriage and family affairs.

- Who should care for the children after a divorce, etc.

- Who are the innocent or guilty parties.

These and many other questions Christ left unanswered. There was no discussion of the many and complex problems that married couples would face in future years. It is evident that He dealt only with the question put to Him by the scheming Pharisees:

"Is it lawful for a man to put away his wife for every cause?" (Mt. 19:3)

Jesus knew very well that some problems married couples would face in the future may be even more subtle and degrading than fornication (drugs, AIDS, domestic violence, alcoholism), yet He did not make any of them a condition for divorce. One thing only can be cause for separation: immorality or sexual sin. Christ understood that divorce is often the fruit of fleshly lusts and impulses that believers are admonished to leave behind when reaching forth for the prize of the high calling of God in Christ Jesus (Phil. 3:14).

THE DISCIPLES' RESPONSE

What was the response of Christ's disciples to their Master's teaching on divorce and remarriage? They were apparently frozen with fear and consternation from His remarks; they muttered, "If the case of the man be so with his wife, it is not good to marry" (Mt. 19:10b). What was the Savior's reply? "But He said unto them, All men cannot receive this saying, save they to whom it is given" (Mt. 19:11).

Can anyone honestly disagree with the disciples over their legitimate fear of the risks and eventualities of marriage? Mark's Gospel makes no mention of the disciples' grief over the matter, but added that they raised the question again after they were settled away at home: "And in the house His disciples asked Him again of the same matter" (Mk. 10:10).

According to Mark's report, the disciples viewed the matter as having sufficient importance to warrant further discussions. Were they silent on the issue? No. Like the disciples and their Master, the Church ought to keep this issue alive and open for constant discussion and review. We must present to the world God's plan for the family and be ready to oppose anything that destroys it.

Christ the compassionate One seeks to repair and restore broken marriages, broken homes, and broken hearts. Have you met Him? Meet this great Restorer before you destroy your marriage through divorce. Let Him help you with your family problems; you'll be glad you did. Others have done so before you with great success. In return they have received many blessings from God, so why won't you?

NOTES AND REFERENCES

1. Guy Duty, *Divorce and Remarriage*, (Bethany House Publ.).

Chapter 5

What Is Adultery?

Man needs to understand that the family's happiness and longevity does not consist in law courts or in religious rituals, but in unwavering loyalty to the Word of God. God made ample provision for the security, prosperity, and happiness of marriage and the family through His commandments. The purity and moral stability of the family were unconditionally guaranteed by the seventh commandment: "Thou shalt not commit adultery" (Ex. 20:14).

But what really constitutes the sin of adultery? Different dictionaries not only provide a working definition of the term, but also give an interesting etymological derivation of the expression. Scribner and Webster define the word "adulterate" from the Latin *adulterare* as "defilement, to make inferior or impure by admixture of a poorer substance, to pollute, *to commit adultery.*"

A somewhat good example of adultery is seen when water is poured into milk. The milk is diluted or adulterated, leaving only the appearance of a genuine substance. Similarly, when a third party invades or sexually assaults a marriage, or when passes are made at one other than the lawful spouse, the marriage has been diluted or adulterated; adultery has been committed and the marriage defiled.

Adultery is not only the physical sexual act itself, but also the weakening of a marriage through lusting and flirting with others outside the marriage compact. A spouse in the habit of intimately kissing and fondling others of the opposite sex, squandering love and affection that essentially belongs to his or her mate, has committed adultery, even if sexual intercourse was not involved. Adultery, then, is any act or condition that invades the privacy of a marriage in such a way as to attack and weaken its moral forces and foundation.

Adultery is further defined as "sexual relations between two persons, either of whom is married to another," but in biblical terms, adultery goes well beyond this narrow conception. Under the seventh commandment, it also covers sexual impurities. These include homosexual promiscuities, pornographic overtures, lesbian manipulations, and sexual deviations of every kind. The word "fornication" is sometimes used interchangeably with "adultery" to describe different kinds of sexual sins. In giving fornication its broadest meaning, a study document on divorce and remarriage affirms the following:

A. Persistent indulgence in intimate relationships with a partner of the opposite sex, other than the spouse even though failing short of coitus, is a form of unfaithfulness, bordering on actual adultery and may be contributory to divorce.

B. *Lustful thoughts* which do not result in overt acts or unfaithfulness, should not be considered as grounds for divorce. *Thoughts*, although known to the omniscient God, and capable of being judged by Him, cannot be known by man, nor are they to be considered grounds for divorce.[1]

Naturally no one should be judged or punished only for his thoughts, but when immoral thoughts are translated into action, measures should be taken to prevent repetition. Over and over, the apostle Paul in First Corinthians 5 refers to fornication, and incest in particular, as wickedness and commanded the Corinthian church to remove those who indulged in these crimes from its fellowship. They were not even to eat with them (see 1 Cor. 5:11). Adultery is sexual deception practiced by one or both mates upon the other. It is usually preceded by sexual lust, a sin that is vehemently condemned throughout the Scriptures. (See Proverbs 6:23-26; Romans 1:24-27; 13:14; Second Timothy 3:6; and First Peter 2:11; 4:2.)

But does one single act of adultery completely destroy a marriage? Jay E. Adams declared, "Some erroneously conclude [that] adultery itself dissolves marriage because a new marriage is made, but that is not true, biblically speaking. It is not proper to remarry a couple, if and when forgiveness for adultery is sought and obtained and the two decide to continue to live together. They are still married; forgiveness alone is necessary."[2]

Dr. Richard Dehaan, writing on the subject of divorce, points out that many scholars in the Greek Orthodox tradition believe that *porneia* designates continuous and repeated marital infidelity and that Jesus chose this word instead of *moicheia* (adultery) in order to avoid the possible conclusion that one solitary act is sufficient cause for divorce.[3] Other scholars, however, disagree with this traditional view and recognized the testimony of Matthew that adultery does break the marriage relation. "Jesus was not highlighting a legitimate loophole for divorce, but was sounding a solemn warning concerning adultery. This sin, he warned, has the effect of destroying a marriage and a home."[4]

HOW IS ADULTERY COMMITTED?

The Scriptures warn that the heart is deceitful and desperately wicked (Jer. 17:9). Christ declared that it is in the heart that adultery originates, grows, and proliferates: "But those things which proceed out of the mouth come forth from the heart; and they defile the man. For out of the heart proceed evil thoughts, murders, adulteries, fornications, thefts, false witness, blasphemies" (Mt. 15:18-19); "Whosoever looketh on a woman to lust after her hath committed adultery with her already in his heart" (Mt. 5:28).

Solomon formalized this concept: "For as he thinketh in his heart, so is he" (Prov. 23:7a). Cherishing adulterous thoughts and feelings, and feeding the mind with pornographic images from books, films, and photos, surely loosens your rein of control over the mind and opens the way to the adulterous act. One may argue, "I cannot help thinking the way I do." He may wrongly conclude that he is neither responsible for his thoughts, nor control of his mind. A famous writer said,

> You will have to become a faithful sentinel over your eyes, ears, and all your senses, if you would control your mind and prevent vain and corrupt thoughts from staining your soul. The mind should not be left to dwell at random upon every subject that the enemy of souls may suggest. The heart must be faithfully sentineled, or evils without will awaken evils within, and the soul will wander in darkness. The power of grace alone can accomplish this most noble work.[5]

No one can prevent a bird from loitering above his or her head, but that person can certainly prevent it from building a nest there.

The sin of adultery is not committed in thought only. When a person engages in the sexual act outside of marriage, he or she has committed adultery. Such illicit behavior is often described as either pre-marital or extra-marital sexual activity. Many high-sounding phrases have been coined to disguise this sin, but it remains the same old ugly adultery in the eyes of God; Jesus did not change its label.

The distress and destruction caused by those who commit adultery did not escape the Master's notice: "And the scribes and Pharisees brought unto Him a woman taken in adultery; and when they had set her in the midst, they say unto Him, Master, this woman was taken in adultery, *in the very act*" (Jn. 8:3-4). What was Christ's response to this woman's dilemma? Did He simply forgive the woman's sin and send her away rejoicing without reproof or reprimand? The evidence is to the contrary. Our Lord registered His dissatisfaction with the woman's odious behavior and declared His abhorrence of her sexual sin in the strongest possible terms. "Go, and sin no more," He chided (Jn. 8:11). His remarks indicate that He considered adultery a great sin, but one that could be forgiven nonetheless and cleansed by His own precious blood.

PLUCKING OUT THE LUSTFUL EYE

Because lusting is an activity of the eyes, and the eyes feed the mind with immoral thoughts and images of sinful acts, our Lord commanded, "And if thy right eye offend thee [that is, cause you to stumble through lust], pluck it out, and cast it from thee: for it is profitable for thee that one of thy members should perish, and not that thy whole body should be cast into hell" (Mt. 5:29).

Christ said this near the close of His discussions on divorce (see Mt. 5:28-32). The message is clear: Members of the physical body (the arm, the feet, the eyes, etc.), may cause a believer to stumble and fall from the path of purity and of commitment into fornication and sins of the vilest nature. If the soul is to escape the final judgments of God, these bodily members must either be brought under the control of reason and a sanctified will, or be completely severed from the body. The fires of hell still threaten those who through sensual lust transgress the laws of God.

Some religionists argue that believers are under grace and grace alone, and that grace takes care of the sin problem, but Christ's teachings repudiate that belief. The possiblity of a believer committing sin through a member of his physical body should alarm us. It should place us on a constant soul watch, a constant vigilance, against the inroads of immorality and loose living. It enjoins upon us the strictest moral discipline, and makes us responsible not only for our thoughts and deeds, but also for our destiny. Passively sitting back on the fence hoping that grace alone will prevent us from thinking evil thoughts is folly.

Our bodies and minds must be guarded. They must be brought under the control of reason. The Spirit of God must be at the helm. But man's willingness to cooperate is absolutely essential to this operation. Daily surrender to Christ, the Master Surgeon, is not an option but an undiminished obligation. Jesus warned, "Ye must be born again" (Jn. 3:7b). Paul hinted, "...I die daily" (1 Cor. 15:31). "But I keep under my body, and bring it into subjection: lest that by any means, when I have preached to others, I myself should be a castaway" (1 Cor. 9:27).

CONDEMNATION OF ADULTERY

Throughout the Scriptures adultery is condemned as a sin, or vice, that God hates. Joseph in Egypt considered it to be "great wickedness and sin against God." Escaping from Potiphar's wife, who tried to seduce him into committing adultery with her, Joseph declared, "There is none greater in this house than I; neither hath he kept back any thing from me but thee, because thou art his wife: how then can I do this great wickedness, and sin against God?" (Gen. 39:9).

All of the writers and teachers of the New Testament condemned adultery. Peter refers to some as "having eyes full of adultery, and that cannot cease from sin..." (2 Pet. 2:14). Paul was no less forceful in his condemnation of this evil. "You who say that people should not commit adultery, do you commit adultery? ... You who brag about the law, do you dishonor God by breaking the law? As it is written: 'God's name is blasphemed among the Gentiles because of you'" (Rom. 2:22-24 NIV).

Among the nations, adultery always was considered a serious crime and generally was punished by death. "Law codes of ancient nations inflicted severe penalties for adultery. The famous code of Hammurabi (2000 B.C.) inflicted death upon an adulterer by drowning. The Babylonian and Assyrian codes before Hammurabi were likewise severe."[6] Moses, in the law, commanded that the adulterer should be stoned to death (Deut. 22:21-24).

During Cromwell's ascendancy in England, adultery was punishable by death. "In countries where Jews held positions of power, adultery was punished by flagellation and imprisonment."[7] "Adultery therefore, if fully ascertained, must be punished by death, as a practice subversive to the whole design of the Theocratic consitution."[8]

If all who profess to obey the law of God were free from iniquity, my soul would be relieved but they are not. Even some who profess to keep all the commandments of God are guilty of the sin of adultery.

Why do not men and women read and become intelligent upon these things which so decidedly affect their physical, intellectual and moral strength? God has given you a habitation to care for, and preserve in the best condition for his service and glory. Your bodies are not your own.[9]

Ellen G. White also wrote:

I saw that the seventh commandment had been violated by some who are now held in fellowship by the church. This has brought God's frown upon them. This sin is awful in these last days, but the church has brought God's frown and curse upon them by regarding the sin so lightly. I said it was an enormous sin, and there have not been as vigilant efforts made as there should have been to satisfy the displeasure of God and remove his frown by taking a strict thorough coarse with the offenders.[10]

WHAT ABOUT POLYGAMY?

Some claim that since God permitted polygamy in ancient times, He will condone and even place His blessings upon polygamous attachments today. Polygamy is a man's or a woman's involvement with several spouses at the same time. But God's patience with evil and His kindness toward the sinner should not be mistaken for endorsement and approval of sin. One historian declares, "God has not sanctioned polygamy in a single instance. It was contrary to His will. He knew that the happiness of man would be destroyed by it."[11] God warned early in the Jews' history that a king should not "multiply wives to himself, that his heart turn not away..." (Deut. 17:17). The practice of polygamy turns the mind away from God and from loyal services to Him who has called us to crucify the flesh, the world, and its sinful practices.

In the New Testament, Paul also insisted that monogamy (one husband/one wife) was the norm for Christian leaders: "A bishop then must be...the husband of one wife..." (1 Tim. 3:2). The great apostle knew very well that the Church's influence could be greatly curtailed and its witness muffled by such unseemly behavior.

"What? know ye not that he which is joined to an harlot is one body? for two, saith He, shall be one flesh" (1 Cor. 6:16). Polygamy has always been a sin in the sight of God, one which has had serious consequences. It is more than a cultural norm. To be involved in polygamy is to commit fornication and adultery, sins that are condemned under the seventh commandment: "Thou shalt not commit adultery" (Ex. 20:14).

NOTES AND REFERENCES

1. Study Document on Divorce and Remarriage, North America G.C. S64, 13.

2. Jay E. Adams, *Marriage, Divorce and Remarriage in the Bible* (Zondervan Publishing House, 1980), 6.

3. Richard Dehaun, *Marriage, Divorce and Remarriage*, 13.

4. Stanley A. Ellisen, *Divorce and Remarriage in the Church* (The Zondervan Corporation, 1977), 53.

5. Ellen G. White, *Adventist Home*, 401-403.

6. See *Israel's Laws and Legal Precedents* (Charles Scribners and Sons, 1907).

7. Guy Duty, *Divorce and Remarriage* (Minneapolis, MN: Bethany House Publ.), 90.

8. Fairbairn Patrick, *The Typology of Scripture* (Zondervan). See also Guy Duty, *Divorce and Remarriage*, 90.

9. Ellen G. White, *Marriage and Divorce* Compiled by Leah Schmitke, 105.

10. Ibid.

11. Ibid., 59.

Chapter 6

The Fornication Issue

Why did Jesus deliberately choose the word "fornication" instead of "adultery" to describe the only legitimate ground for divorce?

And I say unto you, Whosoever shall put away his wife, except it be for fornication [porneia], and shall marry another, committeth adultery [moicheia]...." (Matthew 19:9)

But I say unto you, That whosoever shall put away his wife, saving for the cause of fornication, causeth her to commit adultery...." (Matthew 5:32)

For centuries men have debated over the meaning of the word "fornication" as Christ used it in Matthew 19:9 and Matthew 5:32. It is the most crucial point of the whole divorce-remarriage issue. What did Jesus mean when He spoke of fornication as the only ground for divorce? Arguments over a proper definition of the Greek word *porneia* (fornication) have produced a ground swell of controversy among Christians, but the problem has not yet been resolved.

THE CREDIBILITY CRISIS

Matthew's fornication clauses have been challenged by critics who charge that the "exception clauses" are fraudulent because the Gospels of neither Mark nor Luke make any mention of them. None of the other New Testament writers made any exception in Christ's divorce law: not for fornication, homosexuality, bestiality, or any other sex crime. Matthew's critics claim that the fornication exception is an interpolation, a spurious addition to the Scriptures inserted by those who desired to create an exception for themselves.

If this indictment is true, why did God allow such a serious infraction of His holy Word? Why did He permit a deception of this magnitude to be perpetrated upon His people? Furthermore, why did these chiselers supply their interpolations only to Matthew's Gospel and not to Mark's and Luke's?

Answers to these questions and an explanation of the omission in the other Gospels can be found in the distinguished works of many Christian authors and expositors of the Bible. For example, Calvin wrote, "God gave us four Gospels that we might have four views. ... Certainly the Divine Author was not at variance with Himself."[1] Guy Duty wrote, "If each gospel had all the details of the others, what would be the need of the four of them?" This same author also declared:

> When we wish to learn what Christ said on any subject, we must not confine ourselves to one gospel, but must look at the other gospels for other details they may have. Only thus will a subject stand in harmony. Matthew's account of the Sermon on the Mount has 111 verses and Luke's has 29. Would not much be lost if we had only Luke's account? Matthew, Mark and Luke must be studied together, if not, there will be seeming contradictions on many subjects."[2]

But how is it that Matthew alone recorded this exception in Christ's divorce legislation? In *The Watch Tower* is this explanation:

> Catholic authorities generally dismiss this clause on the grounds that parallel accounts in Mark and Luke do not contain it. However, Mc-Clintock and Strong's Encyclopedia explains.

The fuller reconciliation of the passages must be found in the principle that an exception in a fuller document must explain a briefer one, if this can be done without force. Now as divorce for that one reason was admitted by all, Mark and Luke might naturally take this for granted without expressing it.[3]

Many other testimonies can be cited in support of the validity and credibility of Matthew's record of the exception, but sufficient evidence has been put forth for those who believe the truth. There is absolutely no evidence to support the charge of forgery against Matthew's Gospel, and "every document bearing on its face, no evident marks of forgery, the law presumes to be genuine."[4]

FORNICATION DEFINED

One is almost confused by the conglomeration of conflicting views and definitions of the word "fornication." A brief definition of the words "fornication" and "adultery" based on today's English dictionaries is provided here for clarification. However, they should not be taken as final or as the biblical and historical meanings. We want a fuller and more comprehensive meaning of the Greek *porneia* from which our English "fornication" is derived. Christ's use of the word in Matthew 19:9 and the way it is understood in Jewish circles is our main concern.

"In the Bible," says Robert W. Dehaan, "the two Greek words that broadly and explicitly describe sexual sins are "moicheia" which does refer specifically to infidelity involving married people, and "porneia" which covers general sexual immorality."[5]

Moicheia is generally translated as adultery and *porneia* as fornication. Because Christ used the word *porneia* and not *moicheia* in Matthew 19:9, some conclude that if Jesus had meant infidelity in marriage (adultery) He would have used the more specific term *moicheia* instead of *porneia*. Clearly our limited understanding of Christ's statement makes it mandatory for us to diligently search for the fuller meaning of the word.

Webster's Dictionary defines fornication as "sexual intercourse between a man and a woman not married to each other" and adultery as "sexual intercourse between a married person and one other than the lawful spouse."

Of course, these definitions lend themselves only to today's use of these terms. They do not necessarily represent the historical or biblical usages. However, the question still lingers: Why did Jesus use the word *porneia* and not *moicheia* as the exception? Dr. Dehaan in his book *Marriage, Divorce and Remarriage* answers it this way: "Many scholars in the Greek Orthodox tradition, say that 'Porneia' designates continued and repeated marital infidelity, whereas 'Moicheia' would have made one solitary act, the ground for divorce."[6]

Dr. Dehaan's speculation here is in order, but there is still much confusion and mystery surrounding this issue which needs to be clarified. So let us look at a few of the numerous definitions and explanations that have been given to the word "fornication."

1. Pre-marital sexual sin (meaning sexual intercourse before marriage).

2. Remarriage to someone other than the original spouse; for example, a single person marrying a divorcee, or a divorced person remarrying someone other than the original mate.

3. Rabbinically unapproved marriages (marriage that could not be approved by Jewish authorities).

4. Sexual activities involving single persons (as defined in Webster's Dictionary).

5. Adultery, or betrayal of the marriage covenant.

6. Infidelity during betrothal or period of engagement. Joseph attempted to put away his betrothed wife, Mary, for infidelity, but was stopped when the angel stepped in to announce the supreme miracle of the Savior's

birth (Mt. 1:18-20). (A betrothal or engagement was generally held as sacred and binding as the marriage itself.)

7. Sexual abuse in general (any kind of illicit sexual misconduct whether inside or outside of marriage, including homosexuality, bestiality, incest, etc.).

8. Marriage to one of close blood relationship (consanguineous marriages).

9. Marriages of Jews with Gentiles.

Many other definitions for fornication might surface later in our study, but we must discover from this jumble of interpretations just what Jesus meant by "fornication."

FORNICATION—THE PRE-MARITAL SIN CONCEPT

One view of this issue is noted in *The Watch Tower*: "Some argue that since Jesus used the word fornication (Greek-Porneia) and not adultery (Greek-Morcheia) he must have meant some improper act before the marriage that would make the marriage null and void."[7]

Let me illustrate this view. Suppose Ann and Joe are two single individuals who decide to marry each other. They enter a church on Park Avenue and are happily married by Pastor Nuptial, pledging their love to each other before a huge crowd of witnesses. They signed the register, kissed each other, and smiled broadly as they traced their way down the aisle under waves of applause and handshakes.

A few hours pass and then comes the honeymoon. Joe is excited to be with his new bride, but he is destined to disappointment. Ann, his wife, is not a virgin as he had thought. According to the custom, the stained "bed sheet" is the evidence of purity, the proof that a man's wife is a virgin, that she had kept herself inviolate up to the time of her marriage (Deut. 22:13-21). But there was no stained bed sheet that night. Joe is sorely disappointed, but what can he do? He decides to send his wife back to her parents' home with a bill of divorcement in her hands, according to the law of Moses (Deut. 25:1-4).

Joe considers himself not to have been married at all, in spite of the pomp and pageantry displayed at their wedding earlier that day. As far as Joe is concerned, his wife's not being a virgin means that she had committed *fornication*, a sexual sin, sometime prior to their engagement and marriage. He, therefore, considers the marriage null and void and returns Ann to her parents' home. Joe argues that there really was no marriage because Ann had deceived him by giving herself away in some previous sexual act with another man and had failed to confess it to her husband before their marriage, which might have prevented the wedding in the first place.

Whether it is the concealment or the previous sexual act itself that constitutes fornication is not quite clear. Advocates of this doctrine have never fully explained. But if that is what Jesus meant by fornication, it is a rather bizarre and quaint use of the word *porneia*. James M. Boice in his book *Sex, Marriage and Divorce* declares:

> I believe that Jesus was teaching that the only justifiable grounds for divorce was impurity in the woman, discovered on the first night of the marriage, in which case there would be deceit involved in the contract. There are several reasons why I believe this must be so. First, it is the natural implication of the word, for fornication is not the same thing as adultery; and fornication, not adultery, is the word Jesus uses here. Adultery is unfaithfulness after marriage. That is the only possible meaning of the Greek word "Moicheia" and it is suggested most vividly by the Latin phrase from which we have derived our word in English. The phrase is "ad-alterius-torum" which means to another's bed. Thus it is a violation of the marriage.
>
> It must be a union of body with body first of all, which is to say, there must be a valid sexual relationship. This is important. For this reason,

all of the branches of the Christian church have acknowledged that *a marriage has not actually taken place until the sexual union is consummated.* If it does not take place or cannot take place, then the marriage can be annulled as invalid.[8]

Refutations

Jay E. Adams, a modern authority on this subject, does not agree with this interpretation of Christ's words. He wrote:

> The notion that a marriage begins on the honeymoon when sexual relations first occurs not when the vows are taken, is totally foreign to the scriptures. On the former basis, the Pastor would be lying when he says "I now pronounce you man and wife." Nonetheless, a marriage is consummated when a man and a woman exchange vows before God and each other, and they enter into a conventional relationship. The minister officiating at the wedding is telling the truth. The honeymoon union is proper and holy only because the young couple is already married.

> Throughout, the scriptures refer to marriage in itself as something other than, and distinct from sexual union. Marriage authorizes sexual relations. The honeymoon is proper and holy (Heb. 13:4) only because the young couple is already married. Adultery, later on, while exerting

tremendous strains upon the marriage, does not dissolve it. Sexual relations per se do not make a marriage and do not break a marriage.[9]

Guy Duty, a long-time debater of this subject, wrote:

Some teachers claim that fornication in Matthew 5:32 and 19:9 refers only to "premarital sin." They teach that one can divorce a mate for sexual sin committed before marriage, but not for sin after marriage. There are two nationwide radio preachers who say that fornication means only premarital sin, and much trouble has been caused by such factless statements.[10]

Various scholars, including Dollinger, think Christ's statement means fornication committed before marriage. Dr. R.H. Charles, an English scholar, concluded, "Our Lord embraced the side of the Shammites, and Shammai certainly did not teach that fornication has the exclusive sense of premarital sin."[11]

A number of other scholars have drawn similar conclusions. "As Jesus did not give the least indication that he changed the Old Testament meaning of the word fornication, this was the only possible sense in which they (the Jews) could understand it. The meaning of *pre-marital sin only, was never attached to the word.*"[12]

Inevitable Conclusion

Those who insist on the pre-marital sin concept of fornication must inevitably accept the following conclusions:

1. Fornication is exclusively a female crime, and therefore the woman only can be the culprit in a divorce for fornication.

2. Men cannot be charged with fornication since there is no way of detecting pre-marital sexual activities in men; therefore, Christ's divorce ruling does not apply to them.

3. A woman's missing virginity discovered on the night of her honeymoon is sufficient evidence of fornication and therefore legitimate cause for divorce.

4. Jesus meant marital frauds or marital deception of some kind, when He used the word "fornication."

5. Jesus was referring only to a woman concealing a material fact from her husband, one which could be found out only on the night of the honeymoon.

6. A fraud or deception perpetrated upon a husband by his wife's concealing information regarding her pre-marital sex life constitutes fornication.

7. The marriage covenant is valid only after the sex act has been performed and the virginity question settled on the honeymoon night.

8. Divorce in such cases is not necessary to separate the offending wife, since there was really no valid mariage in the first place. Returning her to her parent's home is all that is necessary.

9. The so-called innocent husband will always be free to remarry as he pleases without legal or spiritual road blocks.

The absurdity of such reasoning is nauseating. Is that what Jesus meant by fornication?

Problems

The pre-marital sin concept abounds, but it takes no account of the husband's past, whether or not he was vile, homosexual, or perverted. Only one thing seems important: that his wife be a virgin.

Furthermore, it assumes that Jesus dealt more with a woman deceiving her husband than with a sexual sin committed before marriage. It also assumes that the husband and wife had, prior to their wedding, discussed their own pre-marital sex history. Finally, it conceives that marriage is predicated upon sex.

If this virginity doctrine is true, then what hap pens in the case of a woman marrying a second time?

Does Matthew 19:9 not apply to her as well? How is the virginity test going to be applied? How can her pre-marital sex life be detected? The worst effect of this doctrine, however, is that it allows a husband to put behind him the entire marriage covenant with all the pledges and commitments he made to his wife on their wedding day simply because his wife is not found to be virtuous. Of course, a husband who is not concerned about virginity can plead no other legitimate cause for divorce.

Is not all that a rather bizarre interpretation of Christ's fornication exception? Certainly there must be another, more realistic definition of the word "fornication" to be found. Christ's teaching must go beyond this narrow concept of the Greek *porneia*.

Pre-marital Sin: Already Regulated

If we look at some examples of pre-marital sin in Bible times and how they were dealt with by statute, we can determine whether or not it was necessary for Jesus to make it an issue.

Let me first point out that Moses' law prescribed different penalties for different kinds of pre-marital sins, depending upon the circumstances under which those crimes were committed. For example, one offender might be given the death penalty for a crime while another might simply be asked to marry the woman he assaulted or to pay dowry. Sometimes both the man and the woman, if found out, were put to death. The following three cases explain quite clearly the law on pre-marital sex crimes in Old Testament times.

The first case refers to a man who sexually assaulted an "unmarried" woman, one who was not engaged. The law reads:

And if a man entice a maid that is not betrothed, and lie with her, he shall surely endow her to be his wife. If her father utterly refuse to give her unto him, he shall pay money according to the dowry of virgins. (Exodus 22:16-17)

In this case the seducer was obliged to marry his victim and give her dowry, provided that the parents consented, (see *Clarke's Commentary*, page 131), but the death penalty was not to be administered to this class of offenders.

The second case pertains to a young woman sexually assaulted or raped out in the field or some other solitary place.

But if a man find a betrothed [engaged] *damsel in the field, and the man force her, and lie with her: then the man only that lay with her shall die: but unto the damsel thou shalt do nothing; there is in the damsel no sin worthy of death:* [and I hasten to add, nor of divorce]...*for he found her in the field, and the betrothed damsel cried, and there was none to save her.* (Deuteronomy 22:25-27)

In studying the second case, note carefully the following facts:

1. The rape took place out in the field away from home or friends.

2. The damsel (or young lady) cried but there was none to hear or help her.

3. She is raped, losing her virginity in the process, yet is not guilty of pre-marital sin because she did not consent to the crime. "There is in the damsel no sin" is the biblical verdict (Deut. 22:26).

4. Moses' law upholds the woman's innocence, acquitting her of any wrong doing.

If this case applied to Joe's wife Ann, as mentioned earlier, would it be fair to accuse her of fornication because there was no evidence of virginity on the night of her honeymoon? Would it be proper for Joe to divorce his wife Ann for fornication, citing Christ's law in Matthew 19:9?

It is a different case entirely if the young lady colluded with her captors. Against such collusion the Deutoronomic law reads:

If a damsel that is a virgin be betrothed [engaged] *unto an husband, and a man find her in the city and lie with her; then ye shall bring them both out unto the gate of that city, and ye shall stone them with stones that they die; the damsel, because she cried not, being in the city* [where help was available] *and the man, because he hath humbled his neighbor's wife....* (Deuteronomy 22:23-24)

The woman's sin lies in the fact that she did not cry out for help when help was available. The incident took place in a crowded city and not on a solitary mountainside. She is, therefore, guilty of being an accomplice to the crime and must by law be punished for her part in the affair, not by divorce, but by death. So for this third case, both men and women found guilty of criminal sexual behavior were pelted with stones till they died. A man and woman found guilty of this kind of pre-marital sexual sin would not live to marry each other or to deceive any future marriage partner.

Occasionally, a woman involved in this kind of atrocity was able to escape detection and marry some other mate. But if the husband discovered it on the night of their honeymoon and wanted to make her a public scandal, he could do so. If he did so, the law states that "then they shall bring out the damsel to the door of her father's house, and the men of her city shall stone her with stones that she die..." (Deut. 22:21).

That was the punishment for some forms of pre-marital sexual sins. However, in Ann's case she was divorced not so much for sexual sin, but because it was assumed that she knew of, but connivingly concealed, her non-virtuous status from her husband Joe, an impediment which might have precluded her taking the marriage oath in the first place. Under Moses' law such a woman who hid her non-virtuous condition from her husband was severely punished. She was to be stoned to death (not divorced). (See Deuteronomy 22:20-21.)

So if Moses' law dealt adequately with the pre-marital sin question, what then would be the point in Christ making it an issue? There must be another definition for fornication. Let us examine some of the other interpretations

FORNICATION—REMARRIAGE TO A STRANGER

A very unique but strange definition of fornication was given me by the leader of a certain church whom I interviewed for this book. He defined fornication not as an act, but as a condition in which two persons find themselves married, yet the wife not having "her own" husband, nor the husband "his own" wife.

This condition exists because one or both of the spouses have been previously married and divorced. According to this teaching, no divorced person has the right to remarry. Remarriage places a person in a state or fornication. Since a person is allowed only one living mate, any other would be a stranger to the marriage covenant and therefore not his or her "own" mate. The basis for this conclusion is in First Corinthians 7:2: "Nevertheless, to avoid fornication, let every man have *his own wife,* and let every woman have *her own husband.*"

So the new spouse is not his or her own, since only the original mate can be properly classed as "his own" or "her own." Living together, therefore, would constitute a *state of fornication.*

The leadership of this church insists that that is the only proper definition of "fornication" as Jesus used it in Matthew 19:9. Naturally, this church is vehemently opposed to any form of divorce. They say no divorce for any cause whatsoever; not even for adultery, harlotry, sodomy, incest or any of the other sex crimes mentioned in the Bible. To them, if a divorcee remarries, the marriage is considered "unlawful" and an annulment is in order.

It is perhaps only under these circumstances that this church will grant an annulment or divorce, but with no remarriage thereafter.

FORNICATION—
RABINICALLY UNAPPROVED MARRIAGES

Dr. Dehaan said, "Some tell us that when Jesus used the word fornication, he was thinking of a marriage relationship not approved by the Rabbis, and thus is referred to as a rabinically unapproved marriage."[13] It is in this respect, said Dr. Dehaan, that some scholars understand the use of the word fornication in Acts 15:20.

OTHER DEFINITIONS

"Various authorities recognize that 'Porneia' means unchastity, harlotry, prostitution, fornication, and that at Matthew 19:9, it stands for or includes adultery."[14]

"Our English word 'fornication' from the Latin 'fornix' refers to a brothel or place where Roman Prostitutes made their abode. Every form of unchastity is included in this term fornication."[15]

"The Hebrew word for fornication is 'Zanah' and it is used in Jeremiah 3:1 to depict a married woman committing adultery."[16]

"In Amos 7:17, a married woman is a fornicatress (Zanah)."[17]

"Fornication and adultery are synonymous terms in the scriptures, and they are often interchangeable. The specific meaning must be determined by the context. In the Hebrew and Greek, fornication includes incest, sodomy, prostitution, and all forms of sexual perversions, both before and after marriage."[18]

"Fornication: Prostitution, unchastity of every kind of unlawful sexual intercourse. Adultery appears as fornication, the unfaithfulness of a married woman."[19]

"The word was used to describe all forms of sexual sins whether before or after marriage. It included married or single persons and was not limited to premarital sexual activities."[20]

"Porneia: Illicit sexual intercourse in general. All other interpretations of the term are to be rejected."[21]

"It is my conviction," says Robert Dehaan, "that He [Jesus] was referring to general sexual immorality. In New Testament times 'porneia' was used to cover a wide range of sexual sins; premarital sex, incest, adultery, the relationship of the rabbinically unapproved marriage, and the practice of homosexuality. All of these could fall within the scope of that word 'porneia.' "[22]

Ellisen says that *porneia* is used 26 times in the New Testament in reference to all kinds of sexual immorality.[23]

NOT JUST FOR SINGLES

In Hosea 2:5, *zanah* or fornication is used in reference to Hosea's wife. In Numbers 25:1, the 23,000 Israelites who committed sexual sin with the daughters of Moab (and who died in the wilderness), were not all single persons. Their sin is designated with the word *zanah* (fornication). Paul referred to this same incident in First Corinthians 10:8, noting that they committed fornication: "Neither let us commit fornication, as some of them committed, and fell in one day three and twenty thousand [23,000]."

The apostle referred to married Israelites who committed adultery as well. He said to the married Corinthians, "Neither let *us* commit *fornication* as some of them committed." Did "us" mean only the unmarried or only the single believers? Was Paul addressing only single folks? The sexual atrocities committed in Sodom by married people as well as single people are described in Jude 7 as "fornication": "Even as Sodom and Gomorrha, and the cities about them in like manner, giving themselves over to fornication, and going after strange flesh..." (Jude 7). Was it only the single Sodomites who committed fornication and went after strange flesh?

Paul counseled the Corinthian believers not to keep company with fornicators (1 Cor. 5:9-11). Could they keep company with adulterers then?

The apostle used the word "fornication" to describe consanguineous involvements (close blood relationships, or incest): "It is reported commonly that there is fornication among you, and such fornication as is not so much as named among the Gentiles, that one should have his father's wife" (1 Cor. 5:1).

Ellisen tells us that the word "fornication" is used in the Greek translation of the Old Testament (the

Septuagint) many times as a translation of the Hebrew term *zanah* which meant "playing the harlot."[24] (See Genesis 38:24; Jeremiah 3:1; Ezekiel 16:28 and Hosea 3:3, 5.)

Attorney Elmer Miller of the New York bar made an exhaustive study of the divorce issue from a biblical standpoint and drew the following conclusions: "It would be ridiculous to suppose that in the first century A.D. when illicit intercourse was commonly practiced among gentiles that porneia was used only in the sense of illicit sexual intercourse among unmarried persons."[25]

JESUS' MEANING

In what sense then did Jesus use "fornication"? Our Lord was responding to the Pharisees' question, "Is it lawful for a man to put away his wife for every cause?" (Mt. 19:3b) He was discussing problems in marriage between husbands and wives, not single persons, and in that context used the word "fornication." It is this concept with which many scholars agree.

> When Jesus therefore singled out fornication as a ground for divorce, I believe He had in mind general sexual immorality. ... In fact, every Greek lexicon gives this as the most frequent meaning of the term in actual usage. I might add in passing that if the Lord Jesus had chosen the word *moicheia* (which does refer specifically to infidelity

involving married people) instead of *porneia* (which covers general sexual immorality) to indicate a ground for divorce, He might have given the impression that involvement with a prostitute, sodomy, incest, and other forms of sexual involvement with others did not constitute grounds for divorce."[26]

Perhaps only adultery (sexual relations with others) on the part of the wife constituted grounds for divorce. But what about the husband who is a practicing homosexual? Does Christ's law of divorce on grounds of only fornication apply to him? Can he be divorced for fornication? Homosexuality and all other forms of sexual perversion are described by this one word "fornication." It is in this sense that Jesus used the term. Modern translators understand that and translate *porneia* as marital unfaithfulness, unchastity and immorality.

> *I tell you that anyone who divorces his wife, except for **marital unfaithfulness**, and marries another woman commits adultery.* (Matthew 19:9 NIV)

> *I tell you, if a man divorces his wife for any cause other than **unchastity**, and marries another, he commits adultery.* (Matthew 19:9 NEB)

> *And I say to you, whoever divorces his wife, except for **immorality**, and marries another commits adultery.* (Matthew 19:9 NAS)

Charles R. Swindoll wrote:

This is Christ's personal counsel regarding justification for divorce and remarriage...It is the
Greek word "porneia" from which we get the
term "pornography." Throughout the New Testament it is used repeatedly as a term to describe
illicit sexual activity. In the case of married
partners it would refer to intimate sexual involvement with someone other than one's mate.
This is not simply a case of "quickie sex" on the
sly, a one time only experience. This is "Porneia."
I take this to mean an immorality that suggests
a sustained, unwillingness to remain faithful. I
think of the idea of an immoral life style, an obvious determination to practice a promiscuous
relationship outside of the bonds of marriage.[27]

WARNINGS AGAINST FORNICATION

The apostolic church at Jerusalem handed down
these rulings: "But that we write unto them, that they
abstain from pollutions of idols, and from *fornication...*" (Acts 15:20); "For it seemed good to the Holy
Ghost, and to us, to lay upon you no greater burden
than these necessary things; that ye abstain from
meats offered to idols, and from blood, and from things
strangled, and from *fornication*: from which if ye
keep yourselves, ye shall do well..." (Acts 15:28-29).

New Testament leaders took the threat of a fornication scandal seriously and wrote to the Ephesian

believers: "But fornication, and all uncleanness...let it not be once named among you, as becometh saints. ... For this ye know, that no whoremonger, nor unclean person...hath any inheritance in the kingdom of Christ and of God" (Eph. 5:3,5).

How to Meet the Temptation of Fornication

1. Understand that fornication is a sin against one's own self (1 Cor. 6:18).

2. Remember that whole cities were overthrown because of fornication (Jude 7).

3. Abstain from it (1 Thess. 4:3; Acts 15:20).

4. Avoid it (1 Cor. 7:2).

5. If it lodges in the heart, uproot it (Mt. 15:19; Mk. 7:21).

6. Flee from it (1 Cor. 6:18).

7. Mortify (or destroy) it (Col. 3:5).

8. Part company with fornicators, whether they be inside or outside of the church (1 Cor. 5:9,11).

9. Remember that fornicators have no inheritance in the Kingdom of God (1 Cor. 6:9).

10. Be careful with the fornicator for, like Esau, he will give away his birthright for the thrill of a moment (Heb. 12:16).

*Follow peace with all men, and **holiness**, without which no man shall see the Lord: looking diligently lest any man fail of the grace of God...lest there be any **fornicator**, or profane person....* (Hebrews 12:14-16)

Recognizing the danger and subtlety of the sin of fornication, Ellen White and other Christian writers have written much to warn our generation.

It was the prevalence of this very sin, fornication among ancient Israel that brought them the manifestation of God's displeasure. His judgments then followed close upon their heinous sin, thousands fell, and their polluted bodies were left in the wilderness to rot.[28]

The moral dangers to which all, both old and young are exposed, are daily increasing. "Satan is making masterly efforts to involve married men and women and children and youth in impure practices."[29] "The liberties taken in this age of corruption should be no criterion for Christ's followers."[30]

"Something besides prayers and tears are needed in a time when reproach and peril are hanging over God's people. The wicked works must be brought to an end."[31] "God will accept nothing but purity and holiness; one spot, one defect in character will forever bar men from heaven with all its glories and treasures."[32]

The words of an old familiar hymn vividly express the yearning of every sincere heart for purity and cleansing:

One thing I of the Lord desire,
For all my paths have miry been,
Be it by water or by fire,
O make me clean, O make me clean.
So wash me thou without within,
Or purge with fire, if that must be,
No matter how, if only sin,
Die out in me, die out in me.[34]

NOTES AND REFERENCES

1. Guy Duty as quoted in *Divorce and Remarriage*, 78, (Bethany House Publ.)

2. Duty, *Divorce and Remarriage*, 79.

3. *The Watch Tower* (May 15, 1988).

4. *Evidence admitted in Courts of Law*, 33-34, (1974,); Duty, *Divorce and Remarriage*.

5. Richard W. Dehaan, *Marriage, Divorce and Remarriage*.

6. Dehaan, *Marriage, Divorce, and Re-marriage*.

7. *The Watch Tower* (May 15, 1988).

8. James M. Boice, *Sex, Marriage and Divorce*, 12.

9. Jay E. Adams, *Marriage, Divorce and Remarriage in the Bible* (Zondervan), 6.

10. Duty, *Divorce and Remarriage*, 52.

11. R.H. Charles, *The Teaching of the New Testament on Divorce* (London, 1921).

12. Duty, *Divorce and Remarriage*, 55.

13. Dehaan, *Marriage, Divorce and Remarriage*.

14. *The Watch Tower* (May 15, 1988).

15. *The International Bible Encyclopedia* Vol. 2, 746.

16. *Student's Hebrew Lexicon* (Davis & Mitchell), 185.

17. *Young's Analytical Concordance*, 452.

18. Duty, *Divorce and Remarriage*, 52.

19. *A Greek Lexicon of the New Testament* (Arndt and Gingrich), 699.

20. Dean Alford, *New Testament for English Readers* (Moody Press), 33.

21. *Thayers Greek-English Lexicon*, 532.

22. Dehaan, *Marriage, Divorce and Remarriage*.

23. Ellisen, *Divorce and Remarriage in the Bible*, 51.

24. Ibid.

25. Elmer Miller, as quoted by Guy Duty, *Divorce and Remarriage*, 59.

26. Dehaan, *Marriage, Divorce and Remarriage,* 12.

27. Charles, R. Swindoll, *Divorce* (Portland, Oregon: Multnomah Press), 14-15.

28. Ellen G. White *Testimonies for the Church* Vol. 2, 451.

29. Ellen G. White, Letter 26D 1877.

30. Ellen G. White, *Adventist Home,* 329.

31. *Review and Herald* (May 17, 1987).

32. White, *Testimonies* Vol. 2, 453.

33. Walter C. Smith, Fred H. Byshe, Old Seventh Day Adventist Hymnal No. 634.

Chapter 7

Planning a Divorce?

EFFECTS OF DIVORCE

What happens when a divorce takes place? Do spouses immediately become separated and single again? Is divorce a simple reversal or cancellation of a marriage?

Can a marriage union reach maturation in a two-hour ceremony? For all practical purposes, the joining in wedlock begins on the wedding day, but the process must continue throughout the life of the couple. Growing into marital harmony and maturity takes time.

As marriage begins the gluing process that unites a man and his wife, so divorce begins the process of dissolution and separation. A court may order an annulment, but a marriage is not suddenly destroyed by a court order. As it took time to unite the couple in marriage, so it takes time to separate them through divorce. A couple, though legally divorced, is still glued to each other by affectionate bonds and covenants which cannot be easily broken.

If divorce destroys a marriage instantly and completely as some claim, then why is the marital hangover from a divorce so intolerable and painful? For a number of divorcees, losing weight and losing face is a daily experience, and the process does not end overnight, but goes well beyond the date of the divorce. How can this mystery be explained?

Apparently the marriage is still alive and well after the divorce; the dissolution agent has not fully accomplished its work in their hearts. The two who were lawfully joined together in marriage will never be wholly freed from the cords that bound them the first time. It might be years before hostility has taken its toll, before revenge destroys mental images, before love is repudiated and the voice of conscience finally dies away. It is at this point that the hardness of heart syndrome manifests itself in the number of repressive measures which one or the other spouse must employ to destroy the old feelings of love and sympathy which they once enjoyed. It is that which makes divorce so painful and nauseating, replete with mental and emotional anguish.

CONSIDER WELL

Before you seriously consider your divorce, ask yourself a few pointed questions: Have I honestly evaluated my own role in the breakup of my marriage? Could I have done better than I did? Am I really as innocent as I claim to be? What good counsel am I refusing in order to carry through this divorce? Will I, in time, regret my decision?

Take a hard look at yourself. You might be amazed to discover that your own hard-hearted, inconsiderate attitude is the real cause of your marital unhappiness. Be honest with yourself as you ponder these questions. The consequences are yours to live with for the rest of your life. Running to the divorce courts cannot be your only option.

Some couples view divorce as a convenient quick fix—the magic solution to all their marital problems, but nothing can be further from the truth. Divorce is not a panacea but a destroyer. There was no divorce in God's original plan. Jesus said, "...from the beginning it was not so" (Mt. 19:8). The apostles and New Testament writers did not consider divorce to be a suitable instrument for resolving marital differences. That is obvious from their consistent silence on the issue. They concentrated mostly on the establishment of happier homes and happier marriages (see Eph. 5:22-33). The Church cannot prosper while its homes and families are stricken with strife and dissension. How can the blessings of God rest upon a home where the partners are constantly at each others throats or where they live like strangers, simply passing each other as silent submarines? Whose idea is this really?

Does the motto on your wall, "Christ is the head of this house, the unseen guest at each meal, the silent listener to every conversation," mean anything to you? If it does, why then do you fight? Why do you take each other to court? Why divorce? Is that the only option? In fact, is there no communcation between you and your unseen guest? As a famous Christian writer said, "You ought to live for the approval of God, the respect of your children and the upliftment of your community."[1]

How can that be attained? It can be achieved through faith in Jesus Christ and the promises of His Word. Christian marriage is not for self-aggrandizement or selfish gratification. True marriage has the glory of God and the happiness of others as its goal.

SOLUTIONS

Selfishness is the root of all marital troubles, but there is a remedy for selfishness, a cure for every sick marriage. It is to be found in laboring unselfishly for the good of others and in evaluating one's own personal attitudes toward his or her mate and family.

Is it not selfish for a spouse to please him or herself without regard to the feelings and desires of the other mate? Biblically, no mate has the right to sacrifice the stability and comfort of his or her home to satisfy selfish desires. Marriage is a partnership. Furthermore, when you planned your divorce, did you think about the irretrievables? Did you consider the many others who would be hurt—children, community, church? What was your main concern, pleasing yourself? Did you ask yourself, "Is this what I really want? Is there no other way? Have I exhausted every possible alternative to save my marriage and my family?"

You alone can stop your marriage from breaking up; you alone can prevent disaster. Seeking professional help is wise, but very often the true solution lies in being pragmatic. That means facing reality, dealing squarely and fairly with your own personality traits. If you change your attitudes, the circumstances around you will also change. When the circumstances change, then certainly the race toward divorce will end.

I am reminded of a couple who recently visited the governor of St. Thomas, V.I., to thank him for helping to save their marriage when he was a practicing attorney. The couple had gone to the attorney's office to seek professional help. They wanted a divorce, but the wise attorney compassionately urged them to go back home and try to patch up their differences. "Try to make your marriage work," he insisted. The pair went back and considered the attorney's wise counsel. Today, 20 years later, they are still married. According to the wife, after leaving the attoney's chambers, they had made some serious adjustments to their personal attitudes and habits. In return their marriage succeeded and has worked beautifully since then. Now that couple boasts that nothing in all the world can separate them from each other. They have matured to full stature in mutual love and understanding.

As you contemplate your divorce action, think well of the conseqeunces for yourself and your family. Remember, you are stepping onto what may be a dark and treacherous road. The waves of depression and despair that usually follow divorce are merciless.

Charles Swindoll, the great preacher, closed his booklet on divorce with these striking words:

Being human and sinful and weak, we are all equipped with a remarkable ability to rationalize. Unless we conscientiously guard against it, when we experience marital difficulties, we'll begin to search for a way *out* instead of a way *through*. Given sufficient time in the crucible, divorce will seem our only option, our long-awaited and much-deserved utopia. And we will begin to push in that direction, at times ignoring the inner voice of God's Spirit and at other times violating the written principles of God's Word. Either is a grievous act.

...To carry out that carnal procedure is to short-circuit the better plan God has arranged for His people and, worse than that, is to twist the glorious grace of God into a guilt-relieving excuse for giving us what we have devised instead of accepting what He has designed.[2]

Still planning your divorce? Who is guiding you in this matter? Have you counted the cost? If things do not work out as you planned them, what then?

NOTES AND REFERENCES

1. Ellen G. White, *Adventist Home*, 267.

2. Charles R. Swindoll. *Divorce*, (Portland, Oregon: Multnomah Press), 21.

Chapter 8

The Evolution of Liberal Divorce

Our liberal divorce culture has been evolving for centuries, and we are now seeing what may be only the tip of the iceberg. A history of the growth and toleration of liberal divorce laws and attitudes dates back to the days of the Caesars.

Caesar

"During the reign of Augustus Caesar (30 B.C.-14 A.D.), laws were passed restricting divorce. The most important of these were the Julian laws conceived by Augustus in his old age to reform the morals of the Romans. The Julian laws brought marriage and divorce under the regulation of the state for the first time in Roman history."[1]

Justinian

"The Justinian code formulated in the 6th century, reflected the Christian ardor of the emperor. Justinian desired that the church's views on divorce should prevail, but this view departed drastically from the will of the people. Women...joined the rest of the populace in protesting stringent church laws. Thus, later Justinian legislation provided a number of allowable grounds for divorce."[2] The march toward liberalism had begun.

Roman Catholic Canon Law

"Canon law provided that upon proof of sufficiently serious grounds presented by the wife or husband, a separation could be granted by the church. These grounds were adultery, extreme cruelty, or withdrawal from the church by one of the partners. An annulment was the only method of securing complete freedom fron one's spouse and the privilege of remarrying. Annulments were granted if it was found that the marriage had violated any of the canonical impediments to marriage. Over the years the canonical impediments came to be interpreted so broadly that some grounds could nearly always be found to terminate successfully the marriage of a person who possessed enough political power or influence."[3]

The Protestant Reformation

"The greater freedom to obtain divorces was paralleled by an increased secularization of marriage.... Martin Luther had stated that marriage is 'an external worldly thing, subject to secular jurisdiction, just like dress and food, home and field.'[4] Marital cases were not generally handled by civil courts following the Reformation...but church government was administered by members of royalty, ruling families and others who possessed secular power. The practice of allowing divorces in these fundamentally secular courts for proven adultery, cruelty, and desertion became commonplace.[4] But although divorces on the continent were being increasingly liberalized, they were still somewhat restricted by the church.

The Puritans

"The Puritan John Milton issued a tract in 1643 *The Doctrine and Discipline of Divorce,* in which he expressed his belief that divorce grounds should include contrariness, defects of disposition, and impediments to personal "solace and peace,." and strongly urged the right of private divorce. In his *Tetrachordon,* published two years later, he examined the phrase from the marriage ceremony, "what therefore God hath joined together, let no man put asunder." Milton wrote, 'Shall we say that God hath joined error, fraud, unfitness, wrath, contention, perpetual loneliness, perpetual discord; whatever lust, or wine

or witchery, threat or incitement, avarice or ambi-
tion hath joined together, faithful and unfaithful,
Christian with anti-Christian, hate with hate, or
hate with love, shall we say this is God's joining?'
many of his fellow Puritans...felt that in advocating
private divorce he had gone too far."[5]. Their conservative opposition to liberalizing divorce laws was
well known. "In England between the years of 1669
and 1850, only 229 divorces were granted, all but 3
or 4 of which were to men.[6] But the drift toward
liberalism was to continue among Protestant leaders.

The Church Fathers

Dr. T.D. Woosely, former professor of Greek and
president of Yale University (1846-71), and chair-
man of the American New Testament committee for
revision of the English version of the Bible (1871-81)
is credited with this statement: "Controversy among
the Fathers as to what the grounds should be on
which divorce could be allowed was continuous, and
changes were frequent. The one ground universally
accepted was adultery on the part of the wife."[7]

The Dictionary of Christ and the Gospels, a standard reference work, spotlights the issue in these
words:

At all periods of the history of Christian teaching, differences of opinion have existed within the
Church as to the practical application of Jesus'
words concerning adultery, divorce, and remarriage. These differences have been stereotyped in

the Eastern and Western branches of the Catholic church. The former takes the more lenient view and permits re-marriage of the innocent...
[The latter denied it.][8]

A new reference work by 36 scholars, *A Companion to the Bible* supports this historical account: "...The Eastern church consistently saw in adultery a legitimate cause of divorce, which permits the remarriage of the divorcee, and that at the Council of Trent the Church of Rome forbore to condemn the Eastern discipline on this point."[9] Jerome, Augustine, Calvin, Luther, Wesley and others expressed themselves similarly on this matter of divorce and remarriage to the people of their time. Martin Luther remarked:

> But I marvel even more that the Romanists do not allow remarriage of a man separated from his wife by divorce, but compel him to remain single. Christ permitted divorce in case of fornication and compelled no man to remain single; and Paul preferred us to marry rather than to burn, and seemed quite prepared to grant that a man may marry another woman in place of the one he has repudiated.[10]

John Wesley commented, "It is adultery for man to marry again...unless that divorce, has been for the cause of adultery; in that only case there is no Scripture which forbids to marry again."[11]

John Calvin

"Though Christ condemns as an adulterer, the man who has married a wife that has been divorced, this is undoubtedly restricted to unlawful and frivolous divorces. An adulterous wife cut herself off as a rotten member of the marriage. It is the duty of the husband to purge his house from infamy. By committing adultery he [the husband] has dissolved the marriage, the wife is set at liberty."[12]

Charles Spurgeon

"Marriage is for life and cannot be loosed except by the one great act which severs its bond...a woman divorced for any cause but adultery, and marrying again is committing adultery before God."[13]

The divorce controversy *has been endless*. Hundreds had written on this subject, and it has been debated by church councils for many centuries, yet multitudes remain perplexed.

The Methodists

"In the 1920's the Methodist Church prohibited ministers from performing marriages for divorced persons unless they were innocent parties in divorce granted for adultery. By the 1960's Methodist ministers were required only to satisfy themselves that the divorced person understood the reasons for the failure of the marriage and was prepared to do better the next time."[14]

Other Protestant denominations have long since relaxed their restraints against the remarriage of divorcees, and contemporary American Judaism has followed suit. The following statement made by a leading Jewish rabbi concerning a desirable uniform divorce law is typical:

> Such a law should be drafted with a sense of the realities of the situation with due regard to the frailties of human nature and the exigencies of modern society. Judaism which always maintained a realistic view with respect to divorce, would be in favor of a liberal divorce law which would safeguard the security of the family, but would provide for the dissolution of an intolerable marriage.[15]

Where is all this liberalism leading us, we ask? The Bible foretold this condescension to liberalism as part of a list of last day signs (see Mt. 24:38-39).

NOTES AND REFERENCES

1. *The Encyclopedia Americana* (Grolier Inc.) Vol. 9, 214.

2. Ibid.

3. Ibid.

4. Ibid., 214-215

5. Ibid., 215.

6. Ibid.

7. As quoted in Guy Duty, *Divorce and Remarriage.* 115. (This information was found for Guy Duty by the Research Service of the *Encyclopedia Britanica* in C.G. Harley, *Divorce* (London) 1921.)

8. *The Dictionary of Christ and the Gospels;* as quoted in Duty, *Divorce and Remarriage,* 112.

9. *A Companion to the Bible* (Oxford Press, 1958), 257; as quoted in Duty, *Divorce and Remarriage,* 113.

10. B.L. Woolf, *Reformation Writings of Martin Luther,* London: Lutterworth Press, 1952) 307; as quoted in Duty, *Divorce and Remarriage,* 118.

11. *A Compend of Wesley's Theology,* (Abingdon Press, 1954), 239; as quoted in Duty, *Divorce and Remarriage,* 120.

12. *Harmony of the Evangelists* "John Calvin" Vol. 2, 383-384.

13. *Spurgeon's Popular Exposition of Matthew,* (Zondervan), 28-29.

14. *Encyclopedia Americana,* Vol. 9, 213.

15. Ibid.

Chapter 9

The Legal Side of Divorce

Divorce has both a legal and a religious aspect. It is important for us to understand the basic marriage and divorce laws of our country as well as the biblical and cultural restrictions.

In the United States, a person seeking a divorce generally must appear incourt to explain why he or she wants to end the marriage. A judge then decides whether to grant a divorce. A few states prohibit remarriage for a certain period after a divorce. But in general, a man and woman may marry again—each other, or someone else after their divorce becomes final.[1]

Some states require a waiting period, either before the divorce hearing, or between the hearing and the date that the divorce becomes final. Such a period gives a couple time to reconsider their decision to get a divorce.[2]

"Each state of the United States has its own divorce laws. But all of the states recognize a divorce granted by the state in which one or both of the spouses are legal residents."[3]

The basic question concerning the validity of a divorce is a jurisdictional one: Is the divorce valid according to the state granting it?

GROUNDS FOR DIVORCE

The state legislature establishes the requirements for a divorce. The grounds differ according to the jurisdiction, and include the following:

1. Habitual drunkenness or drug addiction.

2. Neglect or failure to support.

3. Insanity or idiocy.

4. Conviction of a felony.

5. Imprisonment.

6. Prior marriage.

7. Living apart, or long period of separation.

8. Wife's pregnancy at the time of marriage.

9. Incompatibility.[4]

"The Supreme Court, in *Maynard v. Hill*, 125 U.S. 209 (1888), held that...'if within the competency of the legislative assembly of the territory, we cannot inquire into its motives in passing the act granting the divorce, its will was a sufficient reason for its acting.' "[5]

However, the major grounds for divorce both in Europe and the U.S. are (were) adultery, cruelty, and desertion.[6] The only authorized biblical ground for divorce is adultery. The other grounds mentioned may be legal, but not necessarily lawful.

There has been a gradual shift of emphasis from the conventional grounds for divorce to the more liberal practices. The *Encyclopedia Americana* explains:

> The traditional grounds for divorce in the laws of American states were cruelty, desertion, and adultery. A century ago, most divorces were granted on grounds of desertion and adultery. By 1950 these had become minor grounds, and more than half the divorces in the United States were granted on the grounds of cruelty.

> Although grounds for divorce now differ from one state to the next, certain grounds are found in nearly all states. Among these are abandonment or desertion, adultery, and physical cruelty. ...The

definitions of these terms are given within the law of the state, and may differ from one state to another.[8]

The Major Grounds Defined

Adultery

Adultery is the classic ground for divorce and is recognized by all jurisdictions. It is sexual intercourse by a married person with someone other than his or her spouse. Because of the private nature of the act, direct proof is often impossible. Circumstantial evidence is generally admissible. The minimum requirement is proof by a preponderance of evidence of an adulterous disposition and opportunity plus corroborating circumstances that would convince a person of reasonable discretion that the act has taken place.[9]

Cruelty

Cruelty is the most frequently alleged ground for divorce. Originally, extreme physical pain, harm, or a reasonable apprehension was required. The majority of jurisdictions today hold that there need be no physical violence, but there must be reasonable fear of physical harm. The modern trend includes mental cruelty that makes life miserable and unbearable. This approach is listed in some ten states as a new ground for divorce called indignities to the person. Indignities are a kind of mental cruelty, a habitual course of conduct, putting an unconscionable burden on one of the parties.[9]

Desertion

Desertion is the uninterrupted separation of one spouse from the other without justification or consent for the period prescribed by statute. The husband has the right to determine the family domicile. If the wife unreasonably refuses to follow him, she has deserted him, though *he* moved away. If one spouse, through cruelty or some other misconduct, has made it impossible for the other to stay in the home, he may be guilty of constructive desertion. In some juriodic jurisdictions, even where there is no geographical separation, desertion may consist in an unreasonable refusal of sexual relations. The problems of proof in desertion are the lack of justification for the separation, the absence of consent on the part of the deserted party, the intention of not returning, and the uninterrupted fulfilling of the time limit established by statute—from six months to five years.[10]

DEFENSES AGAINST DIVORCE

Four special defenses are possible in a divorce action: collusion, connivance, condonation, and recrimination.

Collusion

Collusion is a fraud perpetrated on the court by the mutual consent of the parties. They may attempt this fraud by agreeing to an act or to the appearances of an act that would be grounds for a divorce, either by testifying falsely about an act that never occurred, or by suppressing a valid defense. If collusion appears, the court on its own initiative may dismiss the suit and punish the parties—and if he or she is involved, the lawyer also.[11]

Connivance

Connivance is the corrupt consent, expressed or implied, of one spouse to the commission of the other spouse of acts constituting grounds for divorce. The key factor is the evil intent of the conniving spouse and may be implied from active or passive cooperation whether or not the guilty spouse is aware of this facilitating consent. The basic principle involved is *volenti non fir injuria*; to him who consents no injury is done.[12]

Condonation

Condonation consists in a conditional forgiveness for an act that would otherwise be grounds for divorce and a restoration to full marital rights. The conditions are that there is true repentance, the offense will not be repeated, and the offended party will be treated with loving kindness. Forgiveness may be expressed or implied, but it must be based on knowledge of the actual offense. If the offense is repeated or another committed, the presumption of true repentance is rebutted. The original offense revives and can sustain a suit for divorce.[13]

Recrimination

Divorce requires both an innocent and an injured spouse. Recrimination recognizes that one cannot complain of the breach of a contract that he himself has violated. If both parties are at fault, the defense of recrimination is applicable and neither is granted a divorce. The alleged offenses may be of the same character (i.e., adultery), or of a different character (i.e., adultery and desertion). In some states the doctrine of comparative rectitude is used to grant a divorce to the one who has the less fault. The modern trend is away from the defense of recrimination, on the theory that if both parties are at fault, there is greater reason for the dissolution of the marriage.[14]

FAULT AND NO-FAULT DIVORCE

There are basically two kinds of divorce in American law. These are usually referred to as the "fault or adversary" type of divorce and no-fault divorce.

Fault Divorce

The plaintiff in a fault action for divorce must prove to the court that the spouse is guilty of actions specified in the complaint; and that these actions constitute grounds for divorce in the state where the action is brought. If the complaint is contested the spouse has the opportunity of answering the charges. The judge then decides whether the divorce will be granted under what conditions.[15]

Courts traditionally have granted divorce chiefly on fault grounds. These grounds vary, but the most common ones are adultery, alcoholism, desertion, drug addiction, failure to support, imprisonment for felony, and mental or physical cruelty. A person seeking a divorce on fault grounds must prove that his or her spouse committed the fault. For example, a woman seeking a divorce on the ground of desertion must prove that her husband deserted her. The husband may contest (argue against) the divorce but if the wife's proof is accepted, the judge grants her a divorce. The judge also may rule against the wife, if the husband can prove that she committed a legal fault. Also, if the husband can prove that his wife consented to or in any way encouraged his action, then the judge may refuse to grant a divorce.[16]

No-Fault Divorce

People who favor no-faults divorce argue that many marriages fail from causes other than the misconduct of a spouse. Therefore they declare a divorce should be granted for reasons other than a fault.

In 1969, California became the first state to enact a no-fault divorce law.[17] In 1970, the National Conference of Commissioners on Uniform State Laws prepared a Uniform Marriage and Divorce Act (UMDA).

The act provides for no-fault divorce if the court finds that the marriage is irretrievably broken. "Irretrievable breakdown" is defined differently among the states, but generally requires that both partners have lived separate and apart for a period of time that may be as long as 12 or 18 months, and that during that time, they lived in accordance with a separation agreement.[18]

A person seeking a divorce on no-fault grounds, does not try to prove that the spouse committed a wrong. The person simply testifies that their marriage has failed and should be legally ended. In many cases the judge grants a divorce even if the person's spouse objects. (In a no-fault divorce action, neither spouse is considered the guilty party.) Some states have replaced all traditional grounds for divorce with the single no-fault ground of marriage break down. Other states have added this ground to their traditional grounds. The 1969 California law provides only two grounds for divorce: (1) irreconcilable differences—that is, disagreements that cannot be settled and have led to the break down of the marriage, or (2) the incurable insanity of one spouse.[19]

The divorce process is simpler under no-fault laws than under fault laws, therefore in some no-fault states, couples can obtain a divorce without hiring lawyers. This method of obtaining a divorce is sometimes called a do-it-yourself divorce. Some judges oppose this type of divorce because they believe a lawyer is needed to protect the rights of spouses and children.[20]

Until 1970 nearly all states granted a divorce only if an "innocent" spouse brought suit against a guilty one for some wrong. The truth of modern marriage is that most failing marriages are the result of incompatibility rather than one-sided bad behavior.

WHEN DIVORCE IS GRANTED

The primary effect of a divorce is a dissolution of the marriage bond; but a divorce does not leave the parties as if they had never been married. There may be a prohibition against remarriage; a statutory time during which neither party can marry anyone else or a permanent or temporary restraint only on the guilty party. The duty of support may continue after the divorce, either to compensate and provide for an innocent spouse, property settlements, separation agreements, and alimony together with their manifold tax problems, which are a major concern when there is a marital break up.[21]

If the judge grants the divorce, he issues a divorce decree that includes the terms of the divorce, such as custody and financial support of the children, visitation rights for the parent not granted custody, financial support, if any for one of the marriage partners, and division of the property. ...The California family law act of 1969 provides that either husband or wife can be required to support the other, and either or both can be required to support their minor children, depending on the courts judgment.[22]

NOTES AND REFERENCES

1. *The World Book Encyclopedia* (Chicago) Vol. 5, 210a.

2. Adapted from *The World Book Encyclopedia*, 210b.

3. Ibid., 210a.

4. Adapted from *The New Catholic Encyclopedia* 1967 Vol. 4, 932

5. Ibid.

6. Ibid.

7. *The Encyclopedia Americana* (Grolier) Vol. 9, 210.

8. Adapted from *The New Catholic Encyclopedia* (1967). Vol. 4, 932.

9. Adapted from *The New Catholic Encyclopedia*, 932.

10. Adapted from *The New Catholic Encyclopedia*, 932.

11. Adapted from *The New Catholic Encyclopedia,* 932.

12. Adapted from *The New Catholic Encyclopedia,* 932.

13. Adapted from *The New Catholic Encyclopedia,* 932.

14. Adapted from *The New Catholic Encyclopedia,* 932-933.

15. Adapted from the *Enyclopedia Americana,* 210.

16. Adapted from *The Encyclopedia Americana,* 210.

17. See *The World Book Encyclopedia,* 210a.

18. Adapted from *The Encyclopedia Americana* 210.

19. Adapted from *The World Book Encyclopedia* 210a.

20. Adapted from *The World Book Encyclopedia,* 210b.

21. Adapted from *The World Book Encyclopedia,* 210a

22. Adapted from *The Encyclopedia Americana,* 210

Chapter 10

The Innocence Syndrome

Serving as a member of the jury in my own country was often a hair-raising experience. The members of the jury listening to evidence from both sides of a case would sometimes be flabbergasted by the testimony of some of the witnesses. So convincing and persuasive were both sides that at times it seemed impossible to determine who was telling the truth and who was not; who was innocent and who was guilty.

Looking back on those days, one thing to me is certain. Determining innocence or guilt, particularly in a marital dispute, cannot be easy. When a marriage breaks down, accurate information is often sketchy and difficult to obtain from any of the parties. Therefore, proving innocence may be to some degree impossible. However, in most jurisdictions, it is not up to the defendant to prove his or her innocence in a trial; it is the court that must establish guilt beyond any reasonable doubt.

But in a marital case, no court can boast absolute certainty about the innocence or guilt of any of the parties.

Where there is no forthright violation of the marriage covenant, who can determine which partner is really responsible for the demise of the marriage? What principles, if any, can one use to determine whether a husband or his wife is the innocent party in the malfunction of their marriage?

WHO IS REALLY INNOCENT?

There is no absolute criterion for judging innocence. Dr. Robert C. Kistler pinpointed the crux of the matter when he wrote:

> The dichotomy of innocence and guilt may not be as clear as was once supposed. For instance, if a wife withholds sexual intercourse from her husband as a way of getting something from him, or of punishing him for something he did, and in such a situation the husband succumbs to the needs of the flesh through intimacy with another woman, which of the marriage mates is innocent and which is guilty?[1]

Is it honest for a husband to lay claim to innocence when it is his abuse and intolerable treatment of his wife that is the principle cause of her alienation from him? Conversely, should a wife honestly consider herself the innocent party when her delinquency, selfishness, and lack of affection for her husband, compounded by her neglect of home duties and her familiarity with others of the opposite sex, have short-circuited the enjoyable rapport that was once the beacon of their home life?

It may be of significance to note that neither Christ nor the apostles mentioned anything about innocence or an innocent party. Man judges only from external evidence, which of course is often misleading. But God judges the heart and the deeper secrets of life. His evaluation of guilt or innocence must therefore transcend all others.

When one person is labeled innocent and the other guilty, each receives different treatment. Some churches rule against remarriage after divorce for either of the parties, regardless of innocence or guilt (except remarriage to the same mate). Others exclude only the guilty one. He or she is not eligible for remarriage for the rest of his or her life. A guilty spouse who remarries is to be considered an adulterer or adulteress. But the remarriage of the innocent party is considered lawful and morally appropriate.

Do you then wonder why some people tell their tale in such a persuasive manner that they soon win the sympathy and admiration of others, securing for themselves a verdict of innocence while scrupulously concealing their guilt and villainy?

FORGIVENESS—THE OTHER OPTION

Although the innocent spouse has the option to divorce his or her mate, there is absolutely no compulsion in the Word of God for him or her to do so. Charles Swindoll said:

> The faithful mate has the option to leave, but such is not mandatory. I have seen numerous marriages rebuilt rather than ended because the faithful partner had no inner peace pursuing a divorce. How much better to look for ways to make the marriage work, rather than anxiously anticipate evidence that is needed to break off the relationship.[2]

Admittedly, the innocent must wrestle with critical choices, particularly the question of forgiveness.

> Forgiveness may or may not be possible depending upon the people involved. Was the person who committed adultery so overwhelmed in a moment of temptation that he yielded without really wanting to do so? Or did he place himself in the way of temptation so that yielding was inexcusable? These are crucial questions the innocent person must face in the framework of his interpretation of the Bible. ...one cannot always make the clear cut distinction desired. This very factor has led most states to pass no-fault divorce legislation, rather than continue some obviously

dishonest practices that were often perpetrated under the innocent-guilty dichotomy of the adversary system of divorce.[3]

However, when one is forgiven, he or she should do all in his or her power to maintain that forgiveness. He or she should earnestly strive to remove the circumstances that made forgiveness necessary in the first place. When Jesus had forgiven the woman taken in adultery, He commanded her to "go, and sin no more" (Jn. 8:11). She was to change her life style from that moment onward. Forgiveness necessitates change. Ellisen wrote:

> If one's marriage partner is playing the harlot or the tomcat with someone else, it is more of a sin to continue living with that one than to separate. To be submissive to such an arrangement by condoning it, is to be a party to it. One should lay down the law to the erring partner and refuse to continue the union. The sinning partner needs to be severely jolted and reminded of the enormity of his or her crime. God doesn't condone such behavior, and He holds us responsible not to tolerate it either. To be timid here is to promote the abomination that God hates worse than divorce.
>
> In taking this action, however, it should be recognized that reconciliation is the primary desire of God. Though divorce or separation may be required to call a halt to an abominable situation of dual sex, the case may not be entirely lost. Admitting

from the evidence of Jesus' words that divorce is permissible and may be necessary when a partner is unfaithful, the believer who has tasted of God's forgiving grace may want to extend that grace to the partner who not only sinned against him or her, but also against God. He or she may want to go the extra mile in overlooking a fault to fill a need by extending unmerited forgiveness. Such forgiveness, of course, should be based upon proper repentance both to God and to all those involved. It should be a repentance which vows anew the couple's faithfulness to each other in the marriage relationship. Anything less would be an invitation to another extra-marital relationship.

A believer should never conceive of reconciliation as an impossibility unless the other party has remarried or is living in a common-law situation. ...Much can be accomplished by appropriating the spiritual resources God has made available, especially those of prayer and patience. If the situation appears impossible, we are reminded that "with God nothing shall be impossible" (Lk. 1:37). To seek God for reconciliation is to move the miracle-working arm of God. The reconciliation of marriage partners is His will and pleasure.[4]

USE WISDOM

At the same time, one should remember that there are three sides to every story, particularly in family disputes. There is the husband's side, the wife's side, and the other side which no one tells. The little patches of information usually omitted from each side of a story are often all that is needed to explain the incident and unfold the mystery of the case.

In a 1976 church council document, the following instructions were given in graphic language:

While the terms guilty and innocent are frequently used in labeling the parties involved in marital break up, the church should recognize that in many cases both partners share responsibility for the failure. The church therefore should use great care in describing the parties to a divorce and avoid judgmental terms: The pastor should try to understand both parties and their respective view points. He should be slow to categorize one as "guilty" and the other as "innocent." At times, serious faults on both sides contribute to the breakdown of marriage. The one considered innocent for example, may have contributed to the other's wrongdoing.[5]

How careful ought ministers to be in becoming involved in the divorce-remarriage extravaganzas of this age? When in doubt, a pastor would do well to pursue a "hands off" policy rather than allowing a chance for his or her ministry and church to be defiled by scandal.

No wise pastor will rush into marrying divorcees in his or her church without much prayer and proper consultation with the members of his congregation, who often know more of the local situation than the pastor does. This spiritual leader will conscientiously try to avoid a rift among the parishioners and the kind of public schism that will undermine his or her ability to meet the spiritual needs of his or her flock.

Ministers need much wisdom and intuition in dealing with their members. They should pray earnestly for wisdom to detect deception, and wherever possible, dispose of it by God's grace through the mighty power of the Holy Spirit.

NOTES AND REFERENCES

1. Robert C. Kistler, *Marriage, Divorce, and...* (Review and Herald Publ. Assoc.), 134.

2. Charles R. Swindoll, *Divorce* (Portland, Oregon: Multnomah Press, 1980), 15.

3. Kistler, *Marriage, Divorce, and ...*, 133.

4. Adapted from Stanley A. Ellisen, *Divorce and Remarriage in the Church*, 54-55.

5. Neal C. Wilson "Divorce, Remarriage, and Church Membership." a statement adopted by the 1976 Council of the General Conference of Seventh Day Adventists (S.D.A) 14.

Chapter 11

Different Denominational Viewpoints

One of the original goals of this book was to formalize and publish the views and practices of various denominations concerning divorce and remarriage. Due to limited space, however, it will not be possible to include in this book the results of all the interviews. But, I have chosen to present three of the more dynamic and outspoken organizations for our study here, as well as my own Seventh Day Adventist church views.

ZION ASSEMBLY

On September 3, 1988, I interviewed Dr. Calton Williams, the pastor of the Zion Assembly congregation here in the Virgin Islands. The experience was indeed an inspiring one. Pastor Williams believes that good, hard counseling given to couples before the wedding day is absolutely essential for a stable and lasting marriage. Capsulizing his remarks on divorce and remarriage, the following may be considered his assembly's position on the issue.

1. The Bible does not encourage divorce in any form. Marital difficulties should be resolved through forgiveness and reconciliation, and not through divorce courts. That is what Zion Assembly believes and teaches, this pastor said. If reconciliation cannot be achieved, then a separation might be in order, but divorce is not to be encouraged whatever the circumstance.

2. Ministers of the assembly are not permitted to marry or even officiate at the wedding of divorcees. The pastor pointed out three groups of people, whom he as a clergyman would refuse to marry at any time. They are: believer with unbeliever, divorcees, and teenagers. His refusal to marry the first two groups is based upon his understanding of biblical theology, he said. When asked why teenagers

were singled out with the others, he replied, "It is a matter of personal preference; many teenagers do not really know what they are about."

3. In his teaching on divorce and remarriage, Christ gave no grounds for divorce other than fornication (Mt. 19:9). Zion Assembly believes that the term "fornication" refers to pre-marital sexual activities.

4. The church accepts divorcees as full members provided they are genuinely repentant and submissive to the will of God and to the guidance of the Holy Spirit.

5. Church members who divorce are generally not dropped from membership, but after much counseling, are allowed to carry on their normal functions in the church, except in leadership capacities.

6. Ministers of other denominations are sometimes permitted to use the church's facilities to perform weddings of divorcees, although Zion Assembly may have reservations regarding the lawfulness of the marriage.

7. Pastor Williams feels that his function at a wedding is not just ritualistic or formal, but that he as a minister plays an important role in the process of joining the bride and groom

on their wedding day. His role at the altar cannot be merely ceremonial, he argued, but as a pastor it is spiritual. This minister insists that "whom God has joined together" applies also to him, the officiating cleric joining the couple on their wedding day.

8. Finally, Zion Assembly believes in the permanence of marriage and regards that as the standard. But when a marriage has been broken down and its retrieval seems impossible, then for the good of all, some sort of separation might be in order. Divorce should not be the first consideration. The church believes in the principle of reconciliation as the most effective means of resolving marital conflicts.

* * * * * *

THE MORAVIAN CHURCH

Dr. Charles Peters is the general superintendent of the Moravian churches in the U.S. Virgin Islands. On October 22, 1988, I interviewed this able clergyman. Reviewing the tenets of the Moravian Church on the question of divorce and remarriage, he enunciated his church's position as follows.

1. They believe that the majority of people who get married do so with good intentions. These couples really want to live a unique and happy married life, but somehow, through human

error, they lay aside their marriage pledge, "for better or for worse," and become involved in some marital snarl. Since the Moravian Church believes that divorce is a sinful act, the couple should first try reconciliation. They should seek help from the church or from some Christian psychologist or counselor before taking that fatal step.

2. Dr. Peters believed that Jesus laid down a principle of marriage in Matthew 19; but not the law of marriage *per se*. Moravians believe that marriage is indissoluble and can only be rightly disposed of by death. This is the biblical law of marriage, the doctor insisted.

3. Whatever happens to destroy a marriage is the result of human error which is sin, and sin, he said, can be forgiven.

4. "We marry divorcees in our church, but one or both spouses should belong to a Moravian church. This will give the pastor of the congregation some oversight and an opportunity to offer helpful counsel and care to the couple; we would marry a divorced spouse, provided certain conditions are met," he stated. The divorcee should show signs of genuine repentance and the Christian spirit of reconciliation.

5. When questioned regarding the number of times a person may be married and divorced

in the Moravian Church, the pastor replied by chiding "no fault" divorce as a form of prostitution. He concluded that persons who are parading in and out of marriage through divorce are not serious people and therefore are not eligible for marriage in the Moravian Church.

6. The church will be extremely slow and cautious in performing any ceremony that involves the marriage of two divorcees. It can be done, but it won't be easy, he noted.

7. Divorcees must show signs of genuine repentance before they can be accepted into Moravian fellowship; however, no divorcee will be accepted into the Moravian ministry. If one was already a minister when the divorce occurred, then the circumstances will be evaluated accordingly and given the kind of treatment they deserve, but no divorced person need apply for ministry in the Moravian Church.

8. In summary, this church looks at divorce as "undesirable." It has always given reconciliation the final choice. Dr. Peters recited the experience of a couple who filed suit for a divorce after being married for many years. The judge, who knew the couple's affiliation with the Moravian Church, delayed the trial in

order to brief the pastor (Dr. Peters) whom he had known for a long time. The judge asked the pastor to intervene and counsel the couple, and prevent them from destroying their marriage if possible. The pastor responded quickly to the appeal, the marriage was saved, and the couple are now joyfully celebrating their 50th wedding anniversary.

* * * * * *

THE CATHOLIC CHURCH

On Saturday, November 5, 1988, my research team and I met with Catholic Bishop Sean O'Malley in his downtown church office in Charlotte Amalie, St. Thomas, U.S. Virgin Islands. The bishop, a man of great wisdom and charisma, spelled out in some detail his church's historical and current position on the divorce-remarriage issue.

1. By Catholic standards, a valid marriage is one that has been lawfully contracted between two baptized members of any denomination, between two Catholics or two Protestants. Only marriages contracted in a religious ceremony are considered valid by the Catholic Church. The marriage of two Catholics outside of the church, as in a court of law or with a Justice of the Peace, are not valid for Catholic purposes.

2. Of all the major Christian denominations in the United States, Roman Catholic divorce rates are known to be the lowest. That is probably because Catholics generally do not accept divorces. The church considers all valid marriages to be indissoluble. In some traditional Catholic countries, divorce is not permitted under any circumstance. In Italy, however, divorce is tolerated by the church merely for the purpose of dividing family property, etc. "But remarriage in our view constitutes adultery and therefore cannot be tolerated," the bishop declared.

3. A divorce is not the end of a marriage, said Bishop O'Malley. Neither does it give anyone the right to remarry. This fact should be seriously considered by those contemplating divorce and remarriage.

4. Annulment is the process of dissolving an unlawfully constituted marriage. Proper grounds for annulment are in fact lawful impediments for why the marriage should not have been solemnized in the first place. Pressured marriages and conditional marriages are considered unlawful.

5. It is possible for a Catholic to have several annulments in his or her lifetime. If it could be proven that something worthy of annulment

was present at the conception of each marriage, then the church would grant an annulment each time, said the bishop. Therefore, since the conjugal covenant was not properly constituted in the first place, the parties would then be free to remarry. The age of a marriage or the number of children involved does not influence the annulment process if the marriage was wrongly formed from the beginning.

6. When asked what action the church takes against those who willfully violate the church's rules and regulations and proceed to sue for divorce before a court of law, he replied, "It depends on the circumstances. If violence of some kind was involved, then we would look at the case with compassion, giving it all the attention it deserves." When asked how the church deals with those who divorce and remarry several times, his answer was that the church recognizes only the first marriage as being lawful.

7. Fornication is defined by the Catholic Church as sexual relations involving unmarried as well as married people. It is a mortal sin. Persons practicing fornication are not eligible for communion in the Catholic Church. Adultery is defined as sexual sin which involves only married persons. Pauline privileges, such as

those in First Corinthians 7, are recognized between believers, but remarriage is unacceptable according to Catholic standards.

* * * * * *

SEVENTH DAY ADVENTIST

Divorce is no respecter of persons. In spite of the very strong emphasis placed upon Christian morality and Christian witnessing, the Seventh Day Adventist Church has for decades been wrestling with the problem of divorce within its ranks. The church is known the world over for its idealistic, conservative stand on the issue and for the high moral and ethical concepts that it constantly holds before its members.

The following statements set forth the position of the Seventh Day Adventist Church on the subject of divorce and remarriage.[1]

1. "In the Sermon on the Mount, Jesus declared plainly that there could be no dissolution of the marriage tie, except for unfaithfulness to the marriage vow"[2] (Mt. 5:32; see also Mt. 19:9). Marriage is a divine institution. Its Author intended that a home once established should endure forever to be dissolved only at the death of the partners.

2. Although the Scriptures allow divorce for unfaithfulness to the marriage vows, such an

action is not mandatory. Reconciliation is always to be preferred.

3. In the event that reconciliation is not effected, the innocent spouse has the biblical right to secure a divorce and to remarry.

4. A spouse found guilty of adultery by the church shall be subject to church discipline. Even though the transgressor may be genuinely repentant, he or she shall be placed under censure (termination of all church offices held and revoking of right to voice or vote in exercises of the church) for a stated period of time, in order to express the church's abhorrence of such evil. The transgressor who gives no evidence of full and sincere repentance shall be disfellowshiped (expelled from membership).

5. A guilty spouse, who is divorced, does not have the moral right to marry another while the innocent spouse still lives and remains unmarried and chaste.

6. When a divorce is secured by either spouse, or when both mutually secure a divorce on any grounds other than that of "unfaithfulness to the marriage vow," the party or parties securing the divorce shall come under the censure of the church. It is recognized, however, that

sometimes there may be conditions that make it unsafe or impossible for husband and wife to continue to live together. In many such cases the custody of children, the adjustment of property rights, or even personal protection, may make a change in the marriage status necessary. In some civil jurisdictions such a separation can be secured only by divorce, which under these circumstances would not be condemned. Still, neither one has the scriptural right to remarry unless in the meantime the other party has remarried, committed adultery or fornication, or been removed by death.

7. In a case where any endeavor by a genuinely repentant offender to bring his marital status into line with the divine ideal presents apparently insuperable problems, his or her plea for readmittance shall, before final action is taken, be brought by the church through the pastor or district leader to the conference committee for counsel and recommendation as to any possible steps that the repentant one, or ones, may take to secure such readmittance.

8. No Seventh Day Adventist minister has the right to officiate at the remarriage of any person who does not have a scriptural right to remarry.

NOTES AND REFERENCES

1. References to the Seventh Day Adventist position are taken from Seventh Day Adventist Church Manual (1986 ed.), 174-176.

2. *Thoughts from the Mount of Blessing*, 63.

Chapter 12

The Role of the Church

Has the Church a clearly defined role in the social affairs of man? It is inconceivable that an institution as powerful as the Christian Church could function without some form of interaction with the problems of society. What is the Church's specific role in the issue of divorce and remarriage?

No one would deny that Christ was frank and fair with His hearers. Apart from Himself, He offered no magical solutions to the problems of man. The Master carefully and conscientiously avoided all deviations from the truth. Jesus did not indicate what stand to take or what actions to initiate against those who err through divorce and remarriage. He delegated this responsibility to His Church. It was the duty of the Church to minister discipline to transgressors and to help them walk in purity and holiness before God (Mt. 18:15-17).

As people filled with the Holy Spirit, they were empowered to act in Christ's stead. He commissioned them to perform binding and loosing operations in His name and through His power (Mt. 16:19). They were authorized to initiate new methods and new policies that could be used to strengthen the Church and its Christian institutions. (The home and school were to be on the Church's list of priorities.)

Naturally this work was not to be left up to chance or speculation, nor was it to be built upon the sophistries of man or some fanciful interpretation of the Scriptures. The disciples were given fundamental principles to guide them in all their endeavors. Our Lord did not seek to enact laws for every situation. Christ knew very well that the problems of society would multiply and become more and more complicated. So He gave His followers a broad mandate with freedom to use their own initiatives and experiences as the circumstances warrant and as the Holy Spirit directs.

AN EXAMPLE

A scenario in the Corinthian church illustrates this principle. Not long after Christ ascended to

Heaven, the Christian community faced one of its greatest challenges involving the traditional family system. Should Christian wives, newly admitted into church fellowship, divorce or separate from their unbelieving husbands who refuse to accept or tolerate the Christian faith? Similarly, should Christian husbands divorce their unbelieving wives? Since light and darkness cannot blend (2 Cor. 6:14), should new converts be encouraged to divorce their unconverted spouses and remarry others in the fellowship? Furthermore, if a husband divorces his wife because of her commitment to Christ, is the wife still bound to him by the one flesh covenant? Has she any further obligations to that marriage?

In this case fornication was not the issue; it was unbelief. If fornication had been the issue, Christ's laws as in Matthew 19:9 could easily have been invoked. Unbelief of one partner was the issue in the Corinthian church, and it elicited from the apostle Paul new rulings and guidelines on marital harmony and behavior that was to guide the Church for all time (see 1 Cor. 7:1-16). However, Paul did not claim to be giving all of the instructions and answers to all of the marital problems. Like Christ, he dealt mainly with the issue at hand. If an unbelieving spouse chooses to desert and divorce his or her mate because of the faith, let him or her depart in peace, says Paul. In such cases a man and his wife are no longer bound by the conjugal covenant (see 1 Cor. 7:15).

In the last days divorce will present the Church with its worst headaches. No issue was ever more stubborn and divisive than that of divorce and re-marriage. The matter of what to do or what not to do with divorcees is a real problem for some church leaders. Good Christian relationships of believers are often destroyed by the ill-advised divorce and remarriage of some of them.

RESPONSIBLE COUNSELING

As in apostolic times, inspired leadership is necessary today to guide our churches in times of crisis to clarify spiritual issues and to compose new policies and guidelines to assist believers in emergencies. Church members should know what to expect if their marriage fails. Leaders must act from a heart of love and compassion for the erring and with a willingness to carry out the divine commission in their church. Their real mission is to seek and save the lost (Mt. 18:11). Mistakes are bound to be made in this venture. If you as a leader do err, then do so on the side of leniency and compassion.

People should not attempt to lump all human problems together, but instead treat each as separate and distinct, recognizing that each has its own peculiar differences and needs. Those in authority should be extremely careful not to turn any away from Christ or from God's open door of mercy. Each divorce case that comes to the vestry for counseling should be treated tenderly with concern for the souls of men, and with the Word of God as the foundation for all such counseling.

Remember that the local church does not exist to promote policies and programs, but to offer God's forgiveness and salvation to all people—including divorcees, harlots, profligates and the like. All are important in God's sight and all come within the Church's scope of ministry.

Although the Church is to vigorously promote and maintain the highest possible moral and spiritual standards, as commanded in the Word of God, its leadership should be careful not to become insensitive to human needs. They should not be so naive as to place principles above people. On the other hand, lowering Christian standards and ideals through false compassion is a travesty.

By taking care of today's family needs we might well be taking care of future generations. Watchman Nee wrote, "If we take good care of the families of the next generation, then we have also taken good care of the church of that generation. If the families of the generation coming up are full of problems, we workers will have to spend our time settling family affairs."[1]

John MacArthur, commenting on the Supreme Court's decision to exonerate his church from scandal, wrote, "I trust that the lawsuit will keep believers ever alert to the need for handling all counseling situations with prayer, biblical discernment, and sensitivity."[2] Prayer, biblical discernment, and sensitivity; these most essential tools are to be a part of the Church's equipment when going forth to minister to the needs of men.

HOLD UP THE STANDARD

Without adherence to biblical principles and without commitment to acceptable standards of Christian behavior, there is no real productivity. Paul urged Ephesian believers to dissociate themselves from their pagan lifestyles which once enslaved them and to adopt the new norms of holy living called for by the truth.

Wherein in times past ye walked according to the course of this world, according to the prince of the power of the air, the spirit that now works in the children of disobedience: among whom also we all had our conversation [or life style] in times past in the lusts of our flesh, fulfilling the desires of the flesh and of the mind.... (Ephesians 2:2-3)

*This I say therefore, and testify in the Lord, that ye henceforth **walk not as other Gentiles walk, in the vanity of their mind,** having the understanding darkened, being alienated from the life of God through the ignorance that is in them, because of the blindness of their*

heart: ... But ye have not so learned Christ; if so
be that ye have heard Him, and have been taught
by Him, as the truth is in Jesus: that ye put off
concerning the former conversation the old man,
which is corrupt according to the deceitful lusts;
and be renewed in the spirit of your mind; and
that ye put on the new man, which after God
is created in righteousness and true holiness.
(Ephesians 4:17-18, 20-24)

In these last days, the Church will face even more monumental social and spiritual challenges. Already marital frauds, violence, and large scale unfaithfulness to marriage vows are the norms of our perverse society. We must respond to these challenges from an earnest desire to do the will of God and to maintain biblical standards among the people.

It is the Church's duty to hold up the divine standards of purity and morality that God has ordained for His people. It is also the duty of the Church to establish rules and policies that assist divorcees and others in their struggle for divine approval and inner spiritual peace. Churches are morally obligated to discuss such sensitive issues with their members, to enlighten the people regarding their church's stand on critical moral issues. If not the Church, then who?

The Lord has provided her with capabilities and blessings, that she may present to the world an image of his own sufficiency and that his church may be complete in him. The church is firmly and

decidedly to *hold her principles* before the whole
heavenly universe and the kingdoms of the world;
steadfast fidelity in maintaining the honor and
sacredness of the law of God, will attract the notice and admiration of even the world, and many
will by the good works which they shall behold,
be led to glorify our father in heaven.[3]

A PLACE FOR COMPASSION

Although some church members bring difficulties
upon themselves by their own injudicious course of
action, God's Church ought not to turn deaf ears to
their cries and pleas for help. God's ministers should
not allow sinners to bleed unnoticed by the wayside.
Granted, some issues will be critical and defiant of
human solutions, but Church leaders must, by new
solutions, keep believers trusting in the mercies of
God and experiencing new, dynamic, daily victories
over sin. Many divorcees are painfully struggling to
gain the victory over old habits and old feelings, over
sin and self. Has the Church no mandate to reach
out to these unfortunate ones?

On the other hand, leaders should be cautious
about assigning church offices to divorcees. Members who have married divorced persons, or those
married to unbelievers, often pose a problem for the
harmony and peace of that church.

In order to maintain tranquility in the ranks, leaders must set the example. Concerning the question

of divorcees holding leadership positions in a church, the 1986 edition of a popular church manual reads:

> When a person who has been involved in divorce proceedings is finally re-admitted to church membership, every care should be exercised to safeguard the unity and harmony of the Church by not giving such a person responsibility as a leader, especially in an office which requires the right of ordination, except by very careful counsel.[4]

A UNIQUE PRIVILEGE

It has been some seven thousand years since creation and perfection. The Church is not perfect; it can only do its best with direction from the Holy Spirit, good judgment, and sanctified reasoning. The Bible gives us broad everlasting principles, but does not tell us what to do in every situation. Using sanctified judgment and divine wisdom, we are to be guided by the Word of God and good ol' common sense. Each divorce case is to be evaluated on its own merit, taking all of the circumstances into consideration, while at the same time conscientiously safeguarding the Church's good name.

God grant His Church anointed vision and renewed vigor to meet the challenges and needs of these confusing times, particularly in the area of divorce and remarriage. Leading men and women out of darkness and depravity into God's marvelous light of purity, morality, and truth is undoubtedly a difficult task, but it is also a unique privilege. Shall the Church not use its God-given authority and vision to help divorcees find security and peace in Christ? Can we any longer afford to neglect our responsibility to these unfortunate citizens?

NOTES AND REFERENCES

1. Watchman Nee, *Do All to the Glory of God*, 44.

2. John MacArthur, *Word of Grace News Letter* 12:1 (1988).

3. Seventh Day Adventist Church Manual (1986 ed.), 175.

4. Ibid., 21.

Chapter 13

The Minister's Role

Pastors, I would be shortsighted if I attempted to complete this book without addressing you, the people who have the responsibility of regularly ministering to divorcees and other unfortunate persons in the community. So I want to take the time to point out some of the ugly pitfalls that you are sure to encounter in the ordinary pursuit of your duties; problems which might be overlooked in the hustle and bustle of things.

POSITION AND IDENTITY

In western lands the gospel minister is a specialist, admired as a paragon of virtue. It is the minister who defines and explains true morality, and in fact is looked upon by some as virtue itself. Mandated to defend the immortal principles for which Christ lived and died, the gospel minister has been promised the empowerment of the Holy Spirit in performing the superhuman task of holding firmly against sin and immorality.

As ministers, it is important that you earn the respect and confidence of the people, but infinitely more important is your gaining the approval of Heaven. A minister's effectiveness is not to be judged by saintly garb or pious appearance. Not even titles of honor like "Reverend" recommend the person. Nothing external can make a pastor a good person. Christ in ministers' hearts and lives must be the true source of strength and influence and the supreme power of their life and ministry.

However, in recent times the laxness of some pastors, who apparently have lost their self-control and self-respect, has done much to demean the ministry and harm the Christian cause. Much effort must now be made if we are to recover lost ground and retain public confidence in this holy office.

DETESTABLE SILENCE

I have never understood why the clergy is so silent on issues of such magnitude as divorce and remarriage. Why there are no dialogues and debates on these moral issues I cannot understand, but I can surely guess: The clergy is with the silent majority, the place where they are most comfortable and contented. However, now is certainly not the time for ministers to be silent on moral and spiritual issues. The high rate of divorce in the nation and in the churches should stir our godly souls to wrath and kindle a desire to warn others of their danger. Charles Swindoll wrote:

> A heavy heart has been my companion, as I have forced myself to address a plague in our society that has reached epidemic proportions. Divorce is occurring in homes where both parties are Christians, often in spite of good counsel, prayer and friends, even against the desires of one of the partners.[1]

For the clergy to be silent now seems cynical and heartless to me, like treason of the highest order.

The absence of dialogue and discussions on the issues of divorce and remarriage has led some to conclude that there is nothing to be violated and no biblical standards to be maintained. Many believe they can marry and divorce as many times as they please, without guilt, because the Church takes no substantive position on these issues. They have come to feel that it is the individual's right to decide what is right and wrong for him or herself in these circumstances (situational ethics).

Is it really true that the Church has no moral standards? Or has it simply reneged on its commitment to those standards? The Church's authority is in Heaven (Mt. 18:18), its God is Holy (Lev. 19:2), the Church itself is holy (1 Cor. 3:17), and its ministers ought to be holy (Tit. 1:8). How then can holy ministers of God allow themselves to be driven into silence? As the saying goes, "All that it takes for evil to triumph is for good men to do nothing."

SPEAK UP AND STAND FAST

The free-for-all liberal theology emanating from some pulpits today is disgraceful. It may be appealing to some, but it surely is the cause of much of the laxness and depravity in our society today. One thing is certain: Fraternizing and compromising with evil has never yielded any real good. We are warned in Scripture that "the wages of sin is death" (Rom. 6:23a). Solomon went a step further when he asked, "Can a man take fire in his bosom, and his clothes not be burned?" (Prov. 6:27). We need to follow Paul's command to Timothy to "reprove, rebuke, exhort with all longsuffering and doctrine" (2 Tim. 4:2b).

Now is the time for ministers and others of good will to raise their holy voices in opposition to evil in all its forms, committing themselves firmly to Christian principles and Bible morality. When the actions and policies of a church seem to diverge widely from the truth, ministers should speak out. They should address all irregularities, whatever their description, in the name of Christ.

Ministers should not capitulate to their flocks either. They are not compelled to yield to all of the pressures or wishes of their sometimes insensitive parishioners, especially when moral issues are involved. You are not obligated to marry everyone who comes to your vestry with an application. You should pray much before consenting to a marriage. You do not need the friendship of every church member in order to stay in the ministry. Of course, to have the support and prayers of all parishioners is comforting indeed, but what you need most is God's approval of your ministry. Respect for the ministry cannot be enhanced by capitulation and cowardice.

Let me also add that, while I do not have any compulsion to criticize the ministry, I simply do not believe that pastors without backbone, who cannot properly discern between compromise and compassion, should continue in the ministry. They should be kindly asked to step aside and leave their post of duty to others more capable of facing the critical challenges of a degenerate and declining society. No church can afford to keep a pastor who cannot fulfill his or her role as the spiritual leader of the people.

MAINTAIN YOUR STANDARDS

Reprimanding persons who have transgressed in the area of divorce and remarriage seems to be a thing of the past. I once attended the wedding ceremony of two divorcees in a local church. Several ministers officiated in a very attractive and colorful ceremony. One pastor charged, "I believe that it is God's will that brother 'X' and sister 'Y' be joined in wedlock today." I later pondered the wisdom and seriousness of such platitudes at the wedding of divorcees. Should not the pastor have been a little more conservative with his compliments? I wondered. Does he know all the facts and circumstances that led to the couple's divorce and remarriage? What in all the world gave the pastor such boldness and assurance of God's approval?

It is also distressing to see the officials who married John Doe to his first wife appear again to marry him the fifth time, with all his previous wives still alive. What makes it more poignant is to hear the cleric repeat: "Whom God has joined together, let not man put asunder."

Has God really been joining all of these wives to this one man? Can ministers be so naive and callous as to be unable to distinguish between right and wrong, between the holy and the profane?

Dr. Kistler tells of a Church of the Nazarene pastor who wrote an article entitled "Church Weddings Are Not For Everyone." The Nazarene minister wrote, "I will not perform the wedding ceremony for persons who are not both by profession and by practice Christians."

He came to this conclusion after having married a number of couples in his church who were not committed to Christ and whose marriages sooner or later crumbled. He asked himself a number of straightforward questions.

Was I called by God to perform marriages for people in the house of the Lord, when those persons had not committed their lives to the Lord? Was I to say prayers for two people who did not pray? Was I to read passages from the Bible to a bride and groom knowing full well that they did not intend to build their homes upon the Bible? Was I to ask these two people to utter promises in the presence of Jesus, when they did not regard Jesus as the Lord of their lives? They gave the Almighty only a nod of attention day in and day out, but on their special day, I, the man of God, was to call forth heavenly beatitudes upon their future: What the couples wanted out of it all was the sanctuary, the noble sound of the organ, the dignified image of the clergyman, the luxury and respectability of a church wedding. Enough of this, I decided. I was being used, the church was being used, God was being used.[2]

From time to time persons will come to your office like a shot from a gun, papers in their hands and ready to be married. But take your time. Don't be confused or intimidated by these circumstances. Take time to investigate the people's background and marital histories. It is your privilege. Furthermore, it is your right to say "no" to any whose circumstances make it difficult for you to marry them with a clear conscience. Lovers are not necessarily ready for marriage just because they request it.

Surely the Church ought to make every effort to point divorcees and others to Christ, the Lamb of

God who takes away the sins of the world (Jn. 1:29). They should open their doors and hearts to all, without discrimination, but there is the other side of the coin. I also believe that every effort should be made to preserve the integrity of the Church, its standards, and its moral values. Everything should be done to discourage members from divorcing each other and to encourage them to seek healing and reconciliation.

A PROBLEMATIC QUESTION

The question of whether or not persons with tangled marital situations may be married in a church or admitted into fellowship is still a problem today. Should weddings be performed in a church without regard to the number of times the couple might have been married and divorced in the past? Should members be apprised beforehand of the status and condition under which a divorcee wedding is to be performed? Surely they ought to be shown how such weddings will not violate the Word of God or the standards of the church. Some divorcee weddings do tend to divide members and create confusion. The schism and gossip that usually results from such weddings is traumatic.

Pastors should avoid becoming too involved in these divorce-remarriage anomalies. If there is doubt regarding the biblical grounds upon which a particular marriage may be solemnized, it is up to the pastor to pursue a "hands off" policy if he or she wishes. However, it might be prudent for him or her to show from the Word of God the reasons for the acceptance or denial of the couple's wedding application. Some couples know very well that their marriage is not in accordance with the Word of God, but to give it respectability and status they press for the wedding to be conducted in a church instead of a court of law.

THE PASTOR AND THE PEOPLE

Is it not the people's right to know just where their pastor and church stand on moral issues, such issues as divorce and remarriage, abortion, racism, and the like? Constant dialogue between the ministry and laity will do much to build confidence and quality relations between church members and their pastor. It will also aid the youth, who must constantly be making wise choices and lasting commitments. They should be encouraged to share in the dialogues and discussions of the church. In this way they will receive the education that will prepare them to be strong moral men and women for Christ, making decisions and judgments based upon the Word of God.

I can certainly understand and appreciate the difficulty some pastors face when dealing with immorality in their churches. One pastor I knew very well, who attempted to discipline a member of his church suspected of living an adulterous life style, was blackmailed and persecuted almost to the point of discouragement. But isn't that what the ministry is all about? The ministry is not a bed of roses. More often, it is a field of thorns. Ellen G. White is quoted as saying, "Those who work in the fear of God to rid the church of hindrances and to correct grievous wrongs...will ever meet with resisting influences from the unconsecrated."[3] That is to be expected, but a loving, caring pastor will neither compromise with sin nor pass it by on the other side. "If wrongs are apparent among his people, and if the servants of God pass on indifferent to them, they virtually sustain and justify the sinner and are alike guilty."[4] To rationalize and compromise is a curse—the perfect formula for self-defeat and humiliation.

IF A MINISTER FALLS

Ministers are not superhuman, but are of like passions (Acts 14:15; Jas. 5:17). They too are sometimes plagued by the same divorce nightmare that assaults others. The struggle against the carnal nature and the flesh is the same for ministers as for all others; perhaps it is even greater because of their profession.

Pastors who become victims of the popular divorce menace should, in my opinion, keep a low profile.

They should not do "business as usual" in the church, however innocent they might claim to be. In fact, a conscientious Christian pastor will on his or her own volition step aside in order to avoid confusion. Restoring a minister's credibility is not an easy task. Ministers who have lost their credibility through divorce and remarriage should step down voluntarily to allow the work of God to advance without impediment. Christian ministers are under intense public scrutiny. Patience with an overindulgent, extravagant ministry that preaches one thing and does another is fast running out. Ministers are accountable for their actions. Morality is still an issue. No pastor can confidently counsel the church members while his or her own divorce-remarriage inhibitions are sticking out for public view. The ministry is a high and exalted calling, and its dignity and professionalism should not be allowed to fall into disrepute because of one person's misfortune. A divorced minister before any congregation is a distinct tragedy.

Thank God that not many clergy find themselves in this predicament. The world needs leaders committed to right principles, heroes of the faith whose tolerance cannot be mistaken for weakness or their patience misjudged for cowardice. They will call sin by its right name and are at heart true to God and to duty.

NOTES AND REFERENCES

1. Charles R. Swindoll, *Divorce* (Portland Oregon: Multnomah Press, 1980), 1.

2 Robert Kistler, *Divorce, Remarriage, and...*, 25.

3. Ellen G. White, *Testimonies*, Vol. 3, 270, 271.

4. Ellen G. White, *Testimonies for the Church* Vol. 3, 265-266.

Chapter 14

Your Own Role

A peaceful home is among the endangered species of our time. It is a coveted enterprise. Mounting waves of contentions, bitterness, and acrimony often make some homes more of a battlefield than a playground. Is your home the ideal, the peaceful habitat where divorce and separation are strangers? Do parents and children act in concert, denying themselves each for the other, and in their pursuit of happiness, perform their duties with fidelity and distinction? Does it display the kind of friendship and cooperation that is so rarely found in society today?

In his letter to the Romans, the apostle Paul argued, "If it be possible as much as lieth in you, live

---

peaceably with all men" (Rom. 12:18). Naturally, this counsel includes the relationship between husbands and wives. Theirs should be a peaceful experience.

Paul's letter to Timothy further underscores his genuine concern for the tranquility and prosperity of God's people: "...that we may lead a quiet and peaceable life in all godliness and honesty. For this is good and acceptable in the sight of God our Saviour" (1 Tim. 2:2-3).

The New Testament makes peace a condition for the continuance of God's presence: "Finally, brethren... live in peace; and the God of love and peace shall be with you" (2 Cor. 13:11); "For the Kingdom of God [to which we belong] is not meat and drink; but righteousness, and peace, and joy in the Holy Ghost" (Rom. 14:17).

"Hearts that are filled with the love of Christ, can never get very far apart."[1]

Richard Walters was right when he portrayed the love of Christ as forgiving love.

When we forgive people who have hurt us, we escape from the top of the hour glass. Forgiving frees us from resentment, from false and unnecessary guilt, and from a thousand forms of bondage in which we trap ourselves. Forgiving has tremendous healing power. It can heal the pain of rejection, the stress and tensions of conflict, the disgust we feel ourselves, and the fear and emptiness which are sometimes our lot. God wants us to live joyously.[2]

Is forgiveness known in your home? Is it welcomed? Or are continued tensions a way of life for you?

FORGIVENESS IS NECESSARY

Forgiveness is like a medicine that brings peace and healing to the human soul. The spirit of forgiveness is the spirit of Christ, who taught His followers to forgive one another not once, not seven times, but seventy times seven (490 times) if necessary (Mt. 18:21-22). "...Forgive, if ye have ought against any..." was the instruction Christ gave His followers (Mk. 11:25).

For some, forgiveness is a lost art, an exercise in futility.

Why can't people learn to forgive? Dr. Richard Walters said, "Forgiving is difficult because it demands unselfishness and we are selfish by nature."[3] There is no place on earth where the spirit of forgiveness is more essential than in our homes. No marriage can long exist without this superlative virtue of forgiveness. For husbands and wives to succeed, they will need to learn the art of forgiving each other all through their marital pilgrimage. Parents must practice forgiving their children and children their parents. There is simply no other route to happiness and tranquility at home.

Recently I conversed with a husband who had divorced his wife because she failed to measure up to his expectations. It seemed he was willing to forgive every one else in the world who had wronged him, except his own dear wife. He divorced her after being married only a few short years. Is it not strange that husbands and wives can talk so glibly about forgiveness when it comes to others, but find it so awfully difficult to forgive each other at home?

Jesus demonstrated His forgiveness for sinners in words that cannot be mistaken, words that still bring tears to human eyes and hearts: "Father, forgive them; for they know not what they do" were His words (Lk. 23:24).

Like God, our forgiveness should be unconditional, complete, free of animosity and grudges, free of coercion and pretense. That is not always easy, I admit, but always possible through Christ.

A husband or wife who hates the other and who cannot forgive, regardless of their piety or profession, do not really know God. They do not understand the nature and slavery of sin; neither do they understand what it means to forgive and be free.

Many marriages end in divorce because the partners never learned to forgive each other. Forgiveness is really not an act but an attitude. It is not an ingredient to be used only once or twice per month; it is a day-to-day essential, an integral part of the Christian's armor. One broadcaster noted, "There are often road blocks within ourselves that prevent us from forgiving." Pride, for example, says, "I don't need to forgive and be reconciled because I don't need this person, I can do without the relationship, I'll just avoid him or her." Henry Ward Beecher explained that the phrase "I can forgive but I can't forget" is only another way of saying "I can't forgive."[4]

IN GOD'S PRESENCE

If self is vigorously suppressed, the home will become the citadel of good will, kindness, and cooperation that God intended it to be from the beginning. Such a home will last, standing the test of time. Furthermore, it will be greatly missed in the community when its inhabitants are gone. Finally, that family will receive God's approval in the day of final reckoning. How is your home? Are you doing everything in your power to head off divorce and to keep the peace?

If you and your spouse cannot dwell peacefully together in your earthly habitation, how will you dwell in your heavenly mansion? The following counsel of the apostle Peter is not only timely but conclusive: "Wherefore, beloved, seeing that ye look for such things, be diligent that ye may be found of Him in peace, without spot, and blameless" (2 Pet. 3:14).

The truly peaceful home is a model, the product of God's presence. When the popular motto "Christ is the head of this house, the unseen guest at every meal, the silent listener to every conversation" is taken seriously, then our homes will experience the peace that passes all understanding. Then there will be no talk of divorce and separation, but harmony, love and mutual understanding.

The Model Home

A successful marriage can scarcely be found,
Where the husband or wife is still around.
The wrath of man, like the weather o'er cast,
Thunders and roars like a great big blast.

The old-fashioned religion that once held sway,
With a song in the morning, and a prayer through the day,
Is all but gone, like a thing of nought,
Except for the few who are still old-fashioned at heart.

But this picture can be changed, if yours would be,
The model of a marriage, the world longs to see,
Where the father is at work, with his hands on the wheel,
The children delightfully treading his heels.

His wife in the kitchen, rowing as hard as she could,
To be ready on time with the family food.
No time to be angry, or even to scold,
Children are happy, doing as they're told.
Mother's fine influence, and daddy's great love,
Make home on earth, like heaven above.

No room for divorce or family feud,
Quarrels not welcomed, nor those who are rude,
It is the place where angels delight to descend,
Where the Spirit of Christ controls and defends.

Myriads out there with their homes broken down,
With broken hearts as well,
Battered women, nervous men,
Children bruised and burned, turned infidel.
No need add more to this ugly list,
this poignant record of human hell.

Give the world a chance to see,
What a delightsome place home can be,
When in Christ the Lord, each heart confides,
Through the greatest storm, that house abides.

James Edmeade, 1993

NOTES AND REFERENCES

1. Ellen G. White, *Adventist Home*, 94.

2. Richard P. Walters, *Forgive and Be Free*, 22.

3. Ibid., 25.

4. Lewis Smedes, Excerpts from *Forgive and Forget* (Harper and Row, 1984).

Appendix A

Definitions

1. *Hardness of heart* (Mt. 19:8):
   Stubbornness, obstinacy, lack of the spirit of forgiveness, A mate's refusal to cooperate to save their marriage. To be unsympathetic. This term also suggests a stoical refusal to yield or reason; a rejection of counsel in favor of one's own opinions.

2. *Fornication:*
   Any unlawful or illicit sexual contact, including rape, homosexuality, bestially, lesbian activities, etc.

3. *Annulment:*
   The termination of a marriage because it was unlawfully contracted from the beginning. In

western countries, annulment may only be granted by a court of law.

4. *Marriage:*
A man and a woman covenanting to accept and live with each other for the rest of their lives. To establish a home and family. To join in wedlock.

5. *Remarriage:*
Marriage after divorce or annulment.

6. *Divorce:*
The legal dissolution of a marriage. The formal cancellation of a marriage contract.

7. *Adultery:*
Extra-marital sexual activity or serious contemplation of it; lust; violation of the marriage bed. (See Matthew 5:28-32.)

8. *Lust:*
An evil desire for something or someone. An overpowering sexual urge.

9. *Legal Separation:*
Temporary separation of a man from his wife by a court of law.

10. *Desertion:*
Abandonment of a mate. To leave one's marriage unattended. In some jurisdictions a spouse deserted for more than one year may file for a divorce in a court of law.

Appendix B

How to Improve Your Marital Happiness[1]

Only in action can love be properly evaluated. Husband and wife should go beyond mere words and express their love for each other in matching deeds. "Love cannot long exist without expression. Let not the heart of the one connected with you starve for the want of kindness and sympathy. Let each give love rather than demand it, be quick to recognize the good qualities in each other."[2]

THE TROTMANS' LIST OF 100 WAYS TO SAY "I LOVE YOU"

FOR HUSBANDS:

1. Say it with words. "I love you" said sincerely to your spouse cannot be improved upon.

2. Write a love letter.

3. Send her flowers for no special reason.

4. Buy her the perfume and cosmetics she loves.

5. Keep her picture in your wallet.

6. Keep her picture displayed in your bedroom as well as in your office if appropriate.

7. Tell her often that she is No. 1 (number one) in your life and behave that way.

8. Make time to be with her regularly.

9. Make sure that her car is always in good condition.

10. Watch her favorite TV program with her.

11. Offer to babysit while she goes out with her girlfriends or to classes.

12. Go shopping with her at your expense.

13. Plan and save for a relaxing vacation to a place she dreams of going.

14. Buy her exotic or sexy lingerie.

15. Ask her about her work for the day after you come home in the afternoon.

16. Back her up in training the children.

17. Develop a loving vocabulary and use it frequently.

18. Boast about her in her presence as well as behind her back.

19. Write and/or phone often when you are away from each other for long periods.

20. Let her know often that you are still happy you married her.

21. Take her out to dinner periodically and plan other romantic interludes.

22. Act as if you are back in your courtship days.

23. Be attentive when she talks to you.

24. Relive the last week before your wedding day.

25. Re-enact all the good and exciting episodes in the first month of your marriage.

26. Give her time for herself.

27. Treat her friends with cordiality and respect.

28. Observe what she wears and be generous with compliments.

29. Treat her as your equal.

30. Give her spiritual leadership and support.

31. Buy a book of love poetry and read for her now and then. Better yet, write her a love poem.

32. Dress to please her when you are going out with her.

33. Care for your health so that she can have you for a long time.

34. Make a will and provide for her generously.

35. Secure life insurance to make sure she is adequately taken care of in the event of your untimely death.

36. Provide labor saving devices for her.

37. Respect her contributions to your discussions.

38. Share your experiences, thoughts, and feelings with her.

39. Cater to her desires and wishes. In your sexual activities, ask her what she likes.

40. Make the times of sexual loving special for her. Be generous with romance.

41. Give her lots of cuddling even when you are not interested in sex.

42. Be sparing with criticism and give it in a loving way.

43. Remember those special days: anniversaries, birthdays, and other special occasions.

44. Take criticism without getting angry.

45. Use her ideas and suggestions freely and let her know that you appreciate them.

46. Give her a massage at the end of a long day.

47. Observe her varying moods and boost her up when she is down.

48. Give her regular, pleasant surprises.

49. Do the household chores you have agreed upon and sometimes help her with hers.

50. Think of ten unique and special ways to show your love for her and use them.

FOR WIVES:

1. Say it with words regularly: "I love you." Men like to hear it too.

2. Keep him well fed with healthy and tasty meals.

3. Keep his clothes clean and ironed. Let him leave your home looking well dressed.

4. Rub his back when he comes home from a hard day's work.

5. Plan a picnic for the two of you to be alone together.

6. Touch regularly out of bed.

7. Share your feelings and experiences with him.

8. Tell him you are proud of him.

9. Acknowledge him as a good provider.

10. Try to show interest in his interests.

11. Pamper him—manicure, pedicure, cream, lotion, etc.

12. Show interest in his work and job.

13. Look for ways to help him get ahead and improve.

14. Boast about him to your friends.

15. Write or call his parents as often as you can.

16. Send him out happy to face the world in the morning.

17. Make yourself attractive to come home to.

18. Remember special days: birthdays, anniversaries, etc.

19. Don't nag.

20. Let the children know in words and action how special their father is to you.

21. Buy him a present he always wanted.

22. Hug him daily.

23. Pray for him daily in his hearing.

24. Keep the bedroom inviting.

25. Let him know you enjoy making love to him.

26. Be willing to try some new experiences.

27. Share your sexual desires and needs with him.

28. Wear sexy nightwear to bed.

29. Be clean and fragrant at bedtime.

30. Cater to his sexual needs.

31. Watch the sports on TV with him.

32. Go to ballgames with him.

33. Be understanding of his moods and know when to be silent and when to ask questions.

34. Compliment him liberally on the positive things he does.

35. Keep his company when he is fixing the car or mowing the lawn.

36. Visit him at his work place. Look attractive so he will be proud.

37. Accept him the way he is. Don't try to change him after the wedding.

38. Don't spend more than he earns. Be economical and thrifty.

39. Be loyal to him at all times.

40. When he comes home exhausted shield him from problems, the telephone, and the children.

41. Keep looking youthful and healthy for him (and yourself).

42. Make yourself lovable on a day to day basis. Act lovable even when you don't feel like it.

43. Go to bed looking beautiful and inviting.

44. Splurge on some sexy underwear.

45. Let him know by your actions that you are not his competitor but his fan.

46. Learn to massage his ego. He will adore you for it.

47. Pretend you don't notice he is getting older.

48. Leave his razors alone and squeeze the toothpaste from the bottom up.

49. When you use his tools be sure to put them back where you found them.

50. Think of ten unique and special ways to show your love for him and use them.

SEXUALITY

Although sex ought not be the most important goal of marriage, the importance of good sexual relations should not be underestimated. Many marriages are failing because of negligence in this area. Paul counsels husbands and wives not to defraud each other; sexual fulfillment is not to be taken lightly (see 1 Cor. 7:4-5). Sexual satisfaction is fundamental to the stability and viability of any marriage. God invented sex, and when it is performed lawfully and in the fear of God, it can be a most pleasurable experience. Not only is the sex act sanctioned in the Scriptures, even the foreplay is symbolized in one form or another (see Song 7:1-6).

Many misconceptions about sex in the minds of some who enter the conjugal covenant need to be corrected. The following article on marriage and sexuality by Jensen Trotman addresses this problem and places sexual relations in the proper biblical perspective.

Marriage and Sexuality

1. Sex is a gift of God to married couples (1 Cor. 7:3-5; Heb. 13:4; Prov. 5:18-19; Gen. 1:27,31; 2:21-25).

2. Ignorance is *not* bliss in sexual matters in marriage. The Bible word often used for sexual

intercourse is "know" (Gen. 4:1,25; 1 Sam. 1:19; Mt. 1:25).

3. Christians are expected to enjoy sex in marriage (Prov. 5:18-19; 1 Cor. 7:3-5; Song of Solomon).

4. Sex is not sinful or dirty, shameful or degrading. Christian couples should rid themselves of this inhibition and see the beauty of sex.

5. Sexual intercourse is intended to be the physical expression of love. The act of sex should be the high point of a full-time love affair between a husband and wife.

6. Both husband and wife should find pleasure and fulfillment in their sexual relations. Sex is not a masculine right and a feminine duty (1 Cor. 7:3-5).

7. Husband and wife should cooperate with each other to make the sex act satisfying and pleasurable for each other. Unselfishness should characterize the relationship.

8. The practice of birth control helps to prevent the fear of pregnancy from robbing the couple of sexual enjoyment.

9. Faithfulness to one's marriage partner is not only God's commandment, but it makes sex more meaningful and enjoyable.

10. Be glad for God's gift of sex and thank Him for it.

SELF-EVALUATION FOR HUSBANDS AND WIVES

If you feel you have been running your home satisfactorily, you might want to grade yourself by using the following score.

How many times in the last 2 months...

I had a good open conversation with my spouse.	1	2	3	4
I prayed for my spouse while at work.	1	2	3	4
I kissed my spouse when one of us left for work.	1	2	3	4
I complimented my spouse in front of others.	1	2	3	4
I listened carefully to my spouse without pre-judging.	1	2	3	4
I surprised my spouse with an unexpected kiss.	1	2	3	4
I accepted criticism graciously.	1	2	3	4
I took time for prayer and Bible study with my spouse.	1	2	3	4
I showed enthusiasm for things that are important to my spouse.	1	2	3	4

I expressed pleasure in our sex life.	1	2	3	4
I visited, called, or wrote my in-laws.	1	2	3	4
I told my spouse I loved him/her.	1	2	3	4

FOR HUSBANDS

I complimented my wife.	1	2	3	4
I did some of the housework.	1	2	3	4
I told my wife I am happy I married her.	1	2	3	4
I took my wife out to eat or swim or play.	1	2	3	4
I concentrated on my wife's enjoyment in love-making.	1	2	3	4
I bought a surprise for my wife.	1	2	3	4
I gave my wife breakfast in bed.	1	2	3	4
I took my wife into my confidence.	1	2	3	4

FOR WIVES

I cooked his favorite food.	1	2	3	4
I was aggressive and passionate in love-making.	1	2	3	4
I stopped watching my favorite TV program to talk with my husband.	1	2	3	4
I tried to make myself more attractive to him.	1	2	3	4

I told my husband I am a happily
married wife.   1 2 3 4

I tried to improve myself.   1 2 3 4

I massaged his back.   1 2 3 4

I did not bring up his past mistakes. 1 2 3 4

SCORE

70-80 — Exceptional. Keep it up.

60-69 — Good. Keep trying.

50-59 — Not bad. Try harder.

40-49 — Room for improvement. You have a lot to catch up on.

MAKING YOUR MARRIAGE A SUCCESS

1. *Guard against selfishness.*
   First you need the subduing grace of God in your heart. "You will both be happy if you *try to please each other.*"[3] "All who are connected with Christ must *guard against selfishness.*"[4]

2. *Avoid contentions.*
   "Satan is ever ready to take advantage when a matter of variance arises...*Let not your marriage life be one of contention.*"[5]

3. *Watch your words.*
   "Be kind in speech and gentle in action, giving up your own wishes; *watch well your words*

for they have a powerful influence for good or evil. Allow no sharpness to come into your voices. Bring into your married life the fragrance of Christlikeness."[6]

4. *Back off.*
"Do not try to compel each other to do as you wish. You cannot do this and retain each other's love."[7]

5. *Be ready for the patience test.*
"Trials will come, it is true even to those who are fully consecrated. The patience of the most patient will be severely tested. The husband or wife may utter words that are likely to provoke a hasty reply, but let the one who is spoken to keep silent. In silence there is safety...'He that is slow to anger is better than the mighty and he that ruleth his spirit than he that taketh a city'. If you refuse to storm or fret or scold the Lord will show you the way through."[8]

6. *Maintain mutual love and respect.*
"There must be love and respect manifested by the parents for one another if they would see these qualities reproduced in their children."[9]

7. *Keep a smiling countenance.*
"Whatever may be his calling and its perplexities, let the father take into his house,

the same smiling countenance and pleasant tones with which he has all day greeted visitors and strangers."[10]

8. *Avoid negatives; continue the early attentions.* "Though difficulties, perplexities and discouragements may arise, let neither husband or wife harbor the thought that their marriage was a mistake or a disappointment. Determine to be all that it is possible to be to each other, continue the early attentions. In every way encourage each other in fighting the battles of life."[11]

NOTES AND REFERENCES

1. The appendix, "How to Improve Your Marital Happiness," was taken from the files of Pastor and Mrs. Jensen Trotman, well-known family counselors of St. Croix, U.S. Virgin Islands. Used by permission.

2. Ellen G. White, *Adventist Home*, 107.

3. Ibid.

4. Ellen G. White, *Adventist Home*, 107.

5. Ibid.

6. Ibid.

7. Ibid.

8. Ibid., 443.

9. Ibid., 178, 216.

10. Ibid., 211, 216.

11. Ibid., 106.

Appendix C

Summary of Christ's Teachings

- In the beginning there was no divorce, no dissolution of the marriage covenant. Marriage between a man and his wife was to be severed only by death (Mt. 19:8).

- Sin (fornication or adultery) is the only acceptable ground for divorce (Mt. 19:9).

- Divorce, even for fornication, is the exception rather than the rule (Mt. 19:9).

- Because adultery, the violation of the seventh commandment, is the only life act that can destroy a marriage, it should be a prime cause for concern among God's people (Mt. 5:27-28).

- Divorce for trivia is frivolous and not in accordance with God's plan for the family. It was allowed under Moses' law because of the hardness of man's heart (Mt. 19:8).

- A man who divorces his wife to make room for another woman commits adultery and leaves the way open for his wife to commit adultery as well. He causes her to sin by putting her away, and therefore ought to share the guilt and penalty for her transgression (Lk. 16:18).

- Adultery may be committed in several ways. It is first conceived in the heart, before the physical act is performed; therefore, it is the heart that must be faithfully garrisoned (Mt. 5:28).

- Marrying a divorcee may result in a life-long adulterous union of husband and wife (Mt. 19:9; Lk. 16:18).

- A man must detach himself from all other alliances, including father and mother, in order to fully unite with his wife. The two then become one flesh (Mt. 19:5).

- Under Moses' law, everything was an exception (Deut. 24:1-4); under Christ, one thing only is the exception: fornication (Mt. 19:9; 5:32).

- A minister may perform a marriage ceremony, but is not necessarily the one who unites a husband with his wife. This is a divine activity; therefore, no frivolous attempt should be made by man to inhibit this process. "What therefore *God hath joined together,* let not man put asunder" (Mt. 19:6b).

- Any marriage can endure if God is at its center and helm (Mt. 19:6; Prov. 3:6).

- Moral discipline is essential to spiritual life and growth. Because the law of God cannot be abolished or compromised in any form, men may opt to become eunuchs (or celebates) for the Kingdom of God. Naturally a person's life style will reflect the quality of his or her choices, which eventually determines his or her destiny (Mt. 19:12).

- The eyes and other members of the body are generally involved in the lust that leads to adultery. Therefore, Jesus warned that these must be brought under strict control and severely disciplined by those bound for the Kingdom of God. The Master taught that the end result of unbridled lust is eternal destruction in the flames of hell (Mt. 5:28-30).

- The great mission of Christ was to redeem men from all sin, including adultery. To the repentant sinner who seeks forgiveness He declares, "...Neither do I condemn thee: go, and sin no more" (Jn. 8:11). "There is therefore now no condemnation to them which are in Christ Jesus..." (Rom. 8:1).

Appendix D

Heading for Divorce? Symptoms, Facts, Questions

SYMPTOMS WORTH CHECKING

Divorce seems to be inevitable for some couples. They could be heading in that direction without even knowing it. By checking themselves against a common list of variables, a couple may know in advance their chances of becoming separated or divorced in a lifetime.

---

1. If you believe that marriage can endure without proper attention and motivation, you are mistaken and might well be heading for divorce without even knowing it.

2. Every business needs personal attention in order to survive and be profitable. How much effort are you expending to keep your marriage fresh, active, and interesting?

3. Are you denying your mate the little attentions and courtesies you promised on your wedding day? If so, you may well be heading for divorce.

4. Do you allow selfishness to obstruct your vision of reality? Are you a selfish person? Is selfishness in control of your life? Do you view others as second rate citizens while you class yourself as first rate?

5. Do you value the company of others more than that of your mate? Do you feel more comfortable with them than with your spouse? You may be heading for divorce.

6. How do you feel about going on long overseas trips and leaving your family behind?

7. Do you plead excuses when your mate asks you for a favor—too busy, too sleepy, too tired—but jump when others ask the same favors?

8. Is your career as important to you as your family? Which one are you prepared to sacrifice if you must?

9. Do you esteem the carnal nature above the spiritual? Do you believe that sex alone can keep a marriage from collapsing? If you do, you do not understand the nature of marriage and may well be heading for your divorce.

10. If you are secretly tampering with the rules of marriage, disregarding purity standards, cheating on your mate, yes, you may expect your divorce.

11. How concerned are you about your spouse's sexual needs—are you doing your best to meet this challenge? Are you withholding yourself from your partner as a way of punishment? Is selfishness controlling the decisions you make in this area of your life?

12. Are you allowing your sex passions to supersede sound judgment, good reasoning, and self control? If so, your marriage is in trouble.

13. Are you easily provoked, irritable, and quick tempered? How well are you fulfilling your duties at home? Do you lack the grace of getting along with others, of making them happy?

14. Some people are perfectionists. Are you one who believes that everyone else in the world

should be as perfect as you are? Are you easily irritated by the imperfections of others? You may be heading for your divorce.

15. Do you view propriety and reserve as essential moral values? Do you enjoy scouting around and flirting with others in the absence of your mate? Do you have the urge to make others, instead of your partner, happy?

16. Are you easily flattered by the opposite sex? Do you revel in self-pity and self praise? Can you function without them?

17. Are you extremely jealous and unable to control your jealousy? To what extremes will you go to protect your possessions?

18. How do you spend family time? Do you idle away the time, watching TV all day? If you do then your marriage will be in trouble sooner or later.

19. Do you lack the virtues of tact, patience, and endurance? Are you a compassionate, caring person?

20. Can you forgive and forget, or do you travel around with hurt and resentment regardless of the consequences? Can you keep the peace? How picky or petty are you?

21. Are you in the habit of spending all of the family's funds, keeping nothing back for the rainy days? Some homes crash because of this indiscretion.

22. Can you cooperate with your mate and with others, or do you always feel that you should be in the lead, winning all of the arguments and having the last word?

23. Do you love to argue until your point is taken and others accept your infallible views? Do you believe that you are always right regardless of the opinions of others?

24. How efficient of a communicator are you? Do you discuss matters thoroughly with your spouse before taking any action?

25. Do you subscribe to the principle of violence or the threat of violence? Is beating and blacking eyes a pastime for you?

26. Is bitterness and acrimony always present in your speech? Do you have control over your self and your words?

27. Can you be corrected by your mate? Will you permit the children to be corrected? If not, divorce may well be your portion.

28. Are you the champion of what is right? Are good judgment, kindness, and compassion elements of your character?

29. How well do you manage under stress?

30. Are you willing to invest quality time with your family or is making money the compulsion of your life? If you focus on money, you may be on your way to the divorce courts.

By changing your own personality you can change the course of your marriage. You cannot change your partner. Do not even try to, but plead earnestly with God to change yourself. Then the natural course of your marriage will change and the march toward divorce will end.

FACTS WORTH KNOWING

- A religiously mixed marriage involves greater risk of divorce than a marriage in which both parties are of the same religion.[1]

- The higher the income, education, and occupational prestige of the couple, the lower is the divorce rate. Divorce rates are higher among the poorer, less educated groups.[2]

- The divorce rate is significantly higher among those who marry young.[3]

- Perhaps as many as one third of all divorces are accounted for by people who are seriously neurotic, emotionally unstable, and psychologically unsuited for marriage.[4]

- Half of all divorces are granted to couples who have been married six years or less. The peak years for divorce are the third and fourth years of marriage, indicating that marital difficulties begin soon after marriage.[5]

- About two-thirds of all divorced women, and three-fourths of all divorced men, ultimately remarry. A third of the remarriages occur within the first year following divorce and more than half take place within two years.[6]

- Remarriages following divorce are at least twice as likely to end in divorce as are first marriages.[7]

- It is commonly accepted among sociologists that there is no necessary relationship between the actual reason for which couples seek divorce and the legal ground they use in a divorce suit.[8]

- Sociologists and other experts agree that a complete, harmonious family is the ideal setting in which to rear children. In the early 1960's more than half of all divorces were granted to couples with one or more children.[9]

- Farmers, one of the non-professional groups, in the U.S. have an extremely low divorce rate.[10]

- Most studies reveal that black couples have a higher divorce rate than white couples.[11]

- Of the three major religious groups in the U.S., Roman Catholics have the lowest divorce rate and Protestants have the highest.[12]

- "A woman's standard of living drops considerably after divorce. Their average standard of living drops 73 percent below what it was during marriage. Older, long-married homemakers often end up with one half to one third of the income their husbands have post divorce."[13]

- "Ex-husbands' standard of living rises an average of 42 percent after divorce."[14]

- "There is no law requiring a husband to pay for a divorce."[15]

- "The costs of a divorce are high. A lawyer usually requires a retainer fee of $1,000 to $7,500 or more up front, and $100 to $300 an hour thereafter. In addition, there will be court costs."[16]

- Couples who do not belong to any denomination have the highest rate of marital disruption.[17]

- Among non-Catholics, Jewish couples have the lowest divorce rates. Among the Protestants,

Episcopalians have the highest rates, and Lutherans the lowest.[18]

- Marriages contracted at an early age are subject to higher divorce rates. The divorce rates for women married under 18 and men under 20 are about one and a half to two times the rate of those married in their 20's.[19]

- "A number of studies show that when children from broken marriages are compared with children from intact marriages, the latter are better adjusted and have better relationships with their parents. ... It can be concluded that marital conflict and disruption are disturbing to children and disorganize their lives."[20]

- Nearly as many Americans receive marriage counseling from the clergy as from all other sources combined.[21]

- It is easier to enter marriage than to terminate one.[22]

- According to the Scriptures, divorce was not part of God's original plan for the human family; it was invented because of the hardness of men's hearts (Mt. 19:8).

- Marrying a divorcee may have grave spiritual consequences; it can be the beginning of a lifetime of adultery. (See Mark 10:11.)

- Moral impurities of any kind will not be allowed to enter into God's Kingdom; absolute holiness is a prerequisite for fellowship with God (Eph. 5:3,5-6).

- Christ's teachings on divorce is the true standard; all should study it carefully before becoming involved in the divorce and remarriage folly of our time.

- Historically serious emotional, social, and economic difficulties usually follow divorce, and the trauma which follows is often grossly underestimated by its victims.

- The behavior of some couples prove beyond any doubt that hatred, resentment, and despair begin to dismantle a marriage long before divorce overturns it.

- God hates divorce, but He is willing to pardon any divorcee who genuinely repents of his or her sin. Nowhere in the Bible is divorce described as the unpardonable sin. (See Malachi 2:14-16 and Matthew 12:31-32.)

- There is no doubt in my mind that moving away from the Creator's safety plan is the principle cause of our current marriage and divorce problems.

Some Statistics[23]

We have become so familiar with the staggering statistics of broken marriages, deserted children, and a decaying society that we are no longer even alarmed by them. Too often we turn aside from these signals, fooling ourselves into believing that all is well. But statistics reveal the sad story that all is not well with the Church or the nation. Soaring divorce statistics are an indicator of a declining society, and if the family fails, the nation tumbles with it.

The number of marriages in the U.S. declined from 2,425,000 in 1985 to 2,400,000 in 1986, a decrease of one percent. The marriage rate was 10.0 per thousand. The 1986 rate was the lowest since 1977.

During the 12 month period ending March 1987, an estimated 2,414,000 couples married, less than one° percent below the number of marriages during the previous 12 month period. The marriage rate for the period ending March 1987 was 10.0 per thousand, one percent lower than the rate of the previous 12 month period.

Year 1985	— 2,425,000	Rate 10.2 per 1,000 population
Year 1986	— 2,400,000	Rate 10.0 per 1,000 population
Year 1987	— 2,414,000	Rate 10.0 per 1,000 population

According to provisional data, 1,159,000 couples were divorced during 1986, two percent less than in 1985. The divorce rate fell from 5.0 per thousand in 1985 to 4.8 in 1986 (the lowest since 1975). During the 12 months ending March 1987, an estimated 1,160,00 couples divorced. The divorce rate was 4.8

Marriages and Marriage rates per 1,000 Population By District of Occurrence Virgin Islands and Each Registration District 1982-1987

Year	Virgin Islands		St. Croix		St. Thomas & St. John	
	Number	Rate	Number	Rate	Number	Rate
1982	1320	13.0	539	10.3	781	15.9
1983	1342	12.9	522	9.7	820	16.4
1984	1417	13.2	476	8.7	941	17.9
1985	1462	13.2	457	8.3	1005	18.1
1986	1811	16.5	552	10.2	1259	22.8
1987	1906	18.0	532	10.2	1374	25.6

Marriage Rates/1,000 Population Virgin Islands and Each District 1982-1987

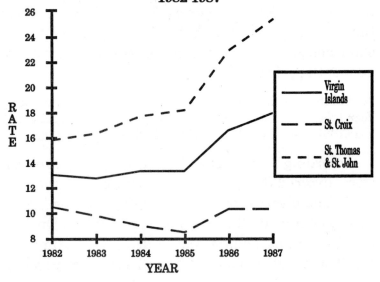

Divorces and Divorce rates per 1,000 Population By District of Occurrence Virgin Islands and Each Registration District 1982-1987

Year	Virgin Islands		St. Croix		St. Thomas & St. John	
	Number	Rate	Number	Rate	Number	Rate
1982	338	3.3	230	4.4	108	2.2
1983	315	3.0	196	3.6	119	2.4
1984	380	3.5	271	4.9	109	2.1
1985	365	3.3	266	4.8	99	1.8
1986	331	3.0	244	4.5	87	1.6
1987	263	2.5	192	3.7	71	1.3

Divorce Rates/1,000 Population Virgin Islands and Each District 1982-1987

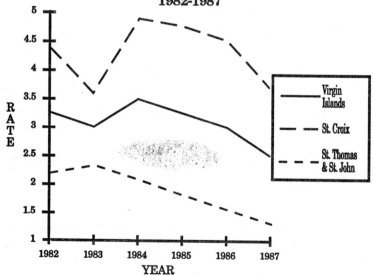

per thousand population, two percent below the figure for the comparable period a year earlier.

Year 1986   — 1,159,000   Rate 5.0 per 1,000 population
Year 1987   — 1,160,000   Rate 4.8 per 1,000 population

QUESTIONS WORTH ASKING

(Suggested answers following.)

1. Should the courts grant divorce to a couple when only one spouse is calling for it?

2. If a woman kisses another man the same way as she would her lawful husband, has she committed adultery? Or as the case may be, a husband kissing another woman?

3. Can a homosexual or lesbian's sexual activities be appropriately labeled adultery? Can a wife divorce her homosexual husband for adultery and vice versa?

4. What is the solution to the problem of one mate being a squanderer and the other a miser?

5. If a person does not love his or her spouse, should that one tell the other so, and what, if anything, can that spouse do?

6. Is a wife bound to consent to her husband's request for an abortion if, to her, such a proposition is unacceptable?

7. Because divorce is so easily obtained today, and some persons are marrying as many as five, six, or even seven times in a lifetime, should the government set limits upon the number of times a person may be married, divorced and remarried in a lifetime?

8. How long can a husband or wife expect to remain angry with each other without the risk of impairing or destroying their marriage?

9. What can be done to help a spouse who is remarkably slow at remembering kindness, but incredibly quick at remembering hurts?

10. For which of these failures does the Bible allow a divorce: (a) Desertion, (b) Incompatibility, (c) Emotional instability, (d) Insubordination, (e) Ill health, (f) Sexual immobility?

SUGGESTED ANSWERS

1. Law courts should be extremely slow in granting divorce or forcing it upon persons who do not want it. "What therefore God hath joined together, let not man put asunder" (Mt. 19:6b).

2. Yes. According to the words of Christ in Matthew 5:28, he or she has by this immoral act committed adultery already in the heart.

3. Yes. A spouse found guilty of homosexual promiscuity is guilty also of adultery and fornication

and therefore is liable to some form of discipline.

4. The solution to these extremes is moderation and cooperation. Tolerance and understanding is a key factor in operating a smooth and harmonious home. Talk freely with each other. Let each present a spending plan.

5. Yes, that person should let his or her spouse know before beginning to demonstrate it. Perhaps a way to improve their relationship would be found.

6. No! In spite of her marriage, a woman's first loyalty is to God. Furthermore, she has certain inalienable rights which should not be denied her.

7. No! Government interference and manipulation of marriage and of the family should not be encouraged under any circumstnces.

8. Bitterness and resentment left unresolved for any period of time can destroy a marriage. Resolve difficulties before bedtime each day, and avoid the risk of marital failure.

9. Great care and tact should be exercised toward such a mate. Love and kidness should be emphasized as often as possible, while keeping personal hurts and annoyances to a minimum.

10. Except for "desertion" under certain circumstances, (1 Cor. 7:10-15), the Bible recognizes none of these as suitable grounds for divorce.

NOTES AND REFERENCES

1. Adapted from *The New Catholic Encyclopedia* (1967) Vol. 4, 930.

2. Adapted from *The New Catholic Encyclopedia*, 930.

3. Adapted from *The New Catholic Encylopedia*, 930.

4. Adapted from *The New Catholic Encyclopedia*, 930.

5. Adapted from *The New Catholic Encyclopedia*, 929.

6. Adapted from *The New Catholic Encyclopedia*, 929.

7. Adapted from *The New Catholic Encyclopedia*, 929.

8. Adapted from *The New Catholic Encyclopedia*, 929.

9. Adapted from *The New Catholic Encylopedia*, 929.

10. Adapted from *The World Book Encyclopedia* Vol. 5, 210c.

11. Adapted from *The World Book Encyclopedia,* 210c.

12. Adapted from *The World Book Encyclopedia,* 210c.

13. Morton Hunt, *Good Housekeeping* (May 1987), 160.

14. Ibid., 160.

15. Ibid., 163.

16. Ibid., 160-163.

17. Adapted from *The Encyclopedia Americana* Vol. 9, 213.

18. Adapted from *The Encyclopedia Americana,* 213.

19. Adapted from *The Encyclopedia Americana,* 213.

20. Adapted from *The Encyclopedia Americana,* 212.

21. Adapted from *The Encyclopedia Americana* 213.

22. Adapted from *The Encyclopedia Americana,* 213.

23. All statistics for this section were gathered from the National Center for Health Statistics, U.S. Department of Human Services, Washington D.C. and the Virgin Islands Bureau of Statistics—St. Thomas, U.S. Virgin Islands.

Conclusion

An Appeal

Dear friend, now that you have read my book, *Before You Divorce,* I trust that you have fully resolved in your heart to, by God's grace, do everything you can to keep your marriage fresh, resilient, and strong; to keep your home safe from the divorce nightmare; to work at having love instead of hate reigning supremely in your home and in your heart; to ensure that your children and others will be blessed by your Godly example.

James Edmeade
Author

About the Author

The author, James J. Edmeade, was born in the British colony of Montserrat, in the West Indies, on November 4, 1929. He attended the government school at Harris where he obtained the highest possible education under the system. In 1945 he migrated to the island of Antiqua, another British colony some 90 miles north of Montserrat, to join his parents in search of profitable employment.

Accepting Christ as his personal Savior in 1948, Mr. Edmeade moved to St. Kitts, and in the 1950's met and married Veronica Merril George, the daughter of a retired police corporal. The union yielded an abundance of seven children: Lester, Hertli, Mirthlyn, Lyris, Dale, Cheryl, and Kenley.

Mr. Edmeade is a professional watchmaker engaged in the watchmaking industry in the U.S. Virgin Islands. His most favored hobbies are music, preaching, teaching, writing, and personal witnessing. His first book, *A Modern Course in Music Theory*, was published in 1976 soon after his return from studies at the Berklee College of Music in Boston, Massachusetts. As a layperson, Mr. Edmeade is deeply committed to lifting Christ up as man's only hope of salvation and renewal.